GENEALOGY 101

Ten Lessons I Wish I Had Known When I Began Researching My Family History

JEDD K. PARKINSON

ISBN: 978-0-578-62309-2

CONTENTS

Introduction   i

1   Talk to Your Elderly Relatives Now!   1

2   Publish Your Work   11

3   Hidden Treasures in Community Records   20

4   Using Online Genealogy Databases Effectively   33

5   Traveling to Your Ancestral Homeland   44

6   The Value of Photos, Video and Audio   60

7   Filing and Organizing Your Digital Records   70

8   Voice Recognition Software and Translation Tools   77

9   The Value of Formal Training   86

10   Find Your Niche   90

INTRODUCTION

I've had a deep interest in my family heritage since I was a young boy. My grandfather, Lee K. Parkinson, was a prolific genealogist and he shared his interest with me. He told me many times that I was the only person among his eight children and 30-plus grandchildren who shared his passion for researching the history of our family, so he included me in his efforts.

Technology played a very minor role in doing genealogy research at the time Grandpa Parkinson introduced me to the work. His efforts were often accomplished through finding and ordering books and records from England, from which he tediously extracted information about our ancestors.

A Mandate from Grandpa Parkinson

A few years before his death, I stopped by to visit Grandpa and he invited me into his office. He had a new stack of Parkinson family genealogy books that he had just received from England. Together we examined the books and then he pushed them across the desk to me and said, "These are yours."

Confused, I asked him why. He explained, "I've done my work. It's now *your* job to finish it."

I was stunned. He had officially passed the torch, but I didn't feel ready nor capable of finishing his work. He was an expert and had been doing genealogy research for decades. He had added more than 28,000 names to our extended family pedigree chart. I loved learning about our family history, but I never imagined it would be *me* surrounded by stacks of records, methodically adding names, dates and other information to pedigree charts.

I told myself that I was way too young to worry about genealogy at that point of my life. That was the work for old people! I was young and still in college!

But, of course, I didn't tell him that. I had too much respect for him and the work he had done. I also knew that if I didn't do it, nobody would. So, I told him I would finish it, and he held me to my word.

My grandfather, Lee K. Parkinson, a prolific genealogist and a well-known oil painter

In the ensuing years I inherited several large boxes that contained all of Grandpa's genealogy records. I'm embarrassed to admit that those boxes sat on shelves in my garage for more than a decade while I was busy finishing graduate school and then pursuing my new career in the tech industry.

However, the responsibility that Grandpa had placed in me, combined with a fair amount of guilt, eventually motivated me to act. One fateful Saturday afternoon I began digging through one of the big boxes, curious to see what it contained. Within a few minutes I found fascinating stories about my ancestors that I had never heard before. I was hooked! My work began in earnest that afternoon, and it continues to this day.

I soon felt an especially strong interest in learning the story of my maternal grandmother's family, the Kaps and Boekwegs, who came to America from Holland between 1899 and 1907. Most of my other ancestral lines had been well-researched by Grandpa Parkinson or other dedicated genealogists in the family, but I was unable to find any meaningful documentation about this Dutch ancestral line.

I did recall my mother and her siblings sometimes talking about Grandma and Grandpa Kap. I knew that they had a huge family and they lived in a very small, humble home with no modern conveniences near the railroad tracks in Ogden, Utah. I remembered the details of their home because my mother and her nine siblings grew up in that same house. I remember Mom saying that Grandma and Grandpa Kap were humble and hard-working. She talked about how they came from Holland and always spoke Dutch. Beyond that, not much was shared and almost nothing was ever written down.

So, I began the process of researching and compiling their life stories, piece by piece. It was an arduous process. I initially thought I would spend a few months assembling a handful of photos along with a summary of their lives, and I would be done. Boy, was I wrong.

Several years later, I'm still researching their line, with one book about their family published, a second nearing publication and a third in the works. Their story was far too interesting and important to be properly researched and summarized within a few months.

This book frequently refers to my work on this Dutch ancestral line since most of the lessons and tips shared here were acquired through my work on that side of my family.

So Why Am I Writing a Book?

As I became serious about genealogy, I quickly realized that everything had changed since the days of looking at books from England with Grandpa Parkinson. Technology was becoming a powerful tool in doing family history research, but I wasn't sure where to begin or how to apply it. Fortunately, I was comfortable using technology, having been a constant user and then a teacher of technology techniques and applications as part of my job in the tech industry.

I soon found, as you might expect, that most of the technology experts were young, but most of the genealogy experts were old. I didn't find anybody who was really good with both technology *and* family history research.

I *did* meet people who helped me learn effective research methods. I also found others who were experts on a range of genealogy archives and information sources. I was extremely grateful for their guidance and assistance.

However, I was unable to find a single person or book that could show me how to do genealogy work *efficiently* and *effectively* through the application of technology. I knew this was what I needed, but it didn't appear to exist.

So, over the subsequent years I invested thousands of hours to figure out these methods and tools on my own, but it was a long, difficult process.

As I became proficient and then began helping others, I realized that they faced the same challenges I had faced, so I started thinking about writing the book that I had wished for. After training and assisting thousands of people with their genealogy research over the ensuing years, I also recognized that I was constantly sharing the same tips, techniques and suggestions with people.

Some of the people I trained learned the lessons quickly, while others wrote things down, but most forgot some or all of what I shared. I was repeatedly asked if I had a book or a manual that included the various techniques and tips.

This book is my attempt to satisfy those requests, with hopes that it will also be useful to those whom I have not personally trained in the past.

As I look back on what I have accomplished since I opened the first of the boxes from Grandpa Parkinson that Saturday afternoon, I have learned so much! But the learning process was often unnecessarily painful. Far too much of what I learned was accomplished through trial and error.

By sharing the 10 lessons and 94 tips that I have employed in my research, I hope that others will be able to avoid many of the pitfalls, frustrations and struggles that I encountered.

Am I Qualified to Write This Book?

This is certainly a fair question. If I were reading this book, this is the first question *I* would ask. All you've learned about me so far is that my grandpa told me it was my job to finish the family history work he began, and I eventually figured out how to do it. What evidence is there that my research approach really works? I would cite the following three items as the best evidence of my qualifications, in addition to the certification I earned in family history research.

1) <u>Efficiency in Acquiring My Personal Collection of Records</u>: At the time of writing this book, my personal genealogy collection includes over 65,000 digitized documents, photos and other records. Those 65,000+ files occupy roughly 200GB on the hard drive of my home computer. In print form, these records would occupy over one million pages. In addition, I have more than 30 hard copy books and thousands of pages of hard copy records, most of which will also be digitized in the future. All of these files were researched, acquired and archived in less than a decade, and the collection has doubled in size over the last two years. The approach I've developed has allowed me to efficiently acquire and organize this vast collection of information in a short time period and keep it manageable.

2) <u>A Combination of Technology and Genealogy Experience</u>: As you would expect, I have spent a lot of time in genealogy libraries and family history gatherings over the past several years. I typically find that my background is quite different from the people I meet in these places, mainly because I was a technology professional before I became serious about family history work.

My tech experience gave me a valuable head start compared to most of the avid genealogists I've met. Of the expert researchers I've worked with, most were much older than I was when they started their work. They typically began their efforts in the old "paper" era and struggled to adapt to a technology-based research approach.

I have had the benefit of using technology applications in my profession on a daily basis since 1997, keeping me aware of the latest tools and solutions that might be useful in family history work. I was also fortunate that Grandpa Parkinson motivated me to begin my work at a relatively young age.

3) <u>Experience in Teaching</u>: I've also been a teacher in one form or another for the past two decades, and that teaching experience has also served me well. I've met some truly amazing experts in various aspects of genealogy research who struggle to transmit their immense knowledge and expertise to others. Why? Teaching effectively is rarely second nature. Becoming an effective teacher and trainer usually takes time, especially if you are teaching people to use a broad range of technologies and techniques that are constantly changing. Many instructors struggle to make technology simple for the average user.

Rarely does a week pass that I don't receive a request to provide family history assistance or training to someone new. The people I have worked with range from teenagers to those in their 80s and 90s. Some have a good foundation in technology while others are afraid of using computers or smartphones. Through these interactions I've gained an understanding of the common struggles and challenges faced by people of all ages in doing their family history work efficiently.

In addition to training people to do family history work, I also have 12 years of experience as a university professor. Furthermore, I've taught classes in the tech industry since 2008, and my standard approach is to find *simple* ways to teach things to others, whatever the topic may be. I have relied heavily on my teaching experience in assembling and then sharing these lessons and tips with others.

Who is My Target Audience?

This book is written for anybody who is interested in researching their family history. I have found that most of the people I work with share three characteristics. They may apply to you as well:

1. They have a strong or even compelling desire to understand their family history, and they feel a special bond with their ancestors. Family history work is not a passive interest for them, but something they feel driven to do. They find great joy and satisfaction in discovering information about their progenitors.

2. They began their research with energy and vigor, and many made good progress at first. But after that initial success, most encountered research obstacles that seemed difficult or impossible to overcome.

3. The obstacles they face, in most cases, could have been avoided if they had employed some basic rules, approaches and techniques in their genealogy work. This should be good news to every reader of this book. I will cover those approaches and techniques in the chapters that follow. In my experience, most people are able to dramatically increase their efficiency and effectiveness after employing these lessons and rules. More importantly, their genealogy work is transformed from being an ongoing series of frustrations to an exciting journey of discovery. There are still plenty of bumps along the road and challenges to overcome, but the overall progress is steady and consistent as they utilize these tips in their work.

Time: Friend or Foe?

As you endeavor to research your family's history, you will likely discover that your primary challenge is *time*. Finding time to do genealogy work is often difficult, partly because family history research is addictive! The more you do the work, the more you want to do. I have met countless people who find themselves awake after midnight on a consistent basis, sifting through old records and not wanting to go to bed because the information is so interesting.

I won't attempt to make this book a lesson in personal time management, but I *will* offer several suggestions of how to efficiently and effectively use whatever time you have available to help you get the most out of your research.

One other aspect of time that is often missed is the fact that the passing of time will eliminate some of the resources available to you. We lose valuable genealogy information each year as elderly family members pass away. With them goes their knowledge, as well as their memories and their stories which were never recorded. In addition, many of these people have their own collections of old family photos, records and stories. Sadly, it is common for such records to be thrown out or lost after they die. Given this risk, I will also touch on some methods for avoiding or at least minimizing such losses of your family's records.

This book includes 94 different tips. I don't expect that every reader will find a use for all 94, or even most of them. However, I have seen many people improve their efficiency and increase their enjoyment of genealogy work by employing just five or ten of these tips, so keep that in mind as you review the various suggestions and ideas. Determine which techniques and approaches are most useful for the work that you are doing and give them a shot!

LESSON 1

TALK TO YOUR ELDERLY RELATIVES NOW!

While the ten lessons contained in this book are not listed in priority order, I believe this first lesson should be the most important, or at least the most *urgent* item on your list.

In my experience, the most valuable way you can spend your limited family history time is in speaking with elderly relatives who have firsthand knowledge of your family's story. I didn't expect that to be true when I began my journey, but I have repeatedly found that if your goal is to discover and document your family's history, there is no substitute for a firsthand interview with an elderly relative. As of 2019 I have interviewed more than 200 elderly relatives and each interview has given me new and useful information.

This may sound like hyperbole, but genealogy work is often a race against time. Don't delay! You will always be able to go back and research public records and archives, but you will never be able to take advantage of an elderly relative's memories and insights once they have passed on.

TIP 1: Interviewing in Person is Always Best

My first suggestion regarding these interviews is to conduct them in person if at all possible. Telephone conversations may also yield a lot of useful information, but an in-person meeting is always the best format.

Meeting with your relatives in person allows you to share and view pictures and to gauge body language. An in-person meeting is also much more likely to produce a comfortable conversation, resulting in a better description and account of memories. Meeting in the relative's home or care center is usually best, but I have also spoken with relatives who preferred to meet at the home of one of their children or another relative. That also works. I even did one interview in a rather noisy Chick-fil-A. I always make myself available to meet wherever and whenever the person is willing to meet with me.

TIP 2: Record Your Interviews

Perhaps the first lesson I learned about interviewing elderly relatives was to always record the interview. My mother and two of her brothers visited one of their great-aunts (Aunt Grace) in 1997. Grace was 96 at the time, but still very sharp mentally. She was known throughout her life for having a remarkable memory, so she was an ideal candidate to share memories of the family's story. She came to America as a young girl, so she was also able to provide a priceless firsthand account of the family's immigration experience.

Aunt Grace was also an outspoken woman who was never bashful about sharing her opinions. That made for a wonderfully entertaining conversation. My mom and my uncles interviewed Aunt Grace for 90 minutes that day, asking her about every ancestor they could think of. I am so grateful that my mother thought to bring along a cassette recorder.

I first listened to that tape several years after it was recorded, and it became the perfect outline for organizing my research of my Dutch ancestors. I have probably listened to the recording 50 times at this point, and I still sometimes find useful little tidbits and hints in the conversation that I had previously missed. As far as I can tell, it is one of only three audio recordings of the first-generation Dutch immigrants in my family, and it is by far the most detailed. Without it, dozens of important facts, memories and stories from our family history would have been lost when Aunt Grace passed away a few years later at age 100.

One more anecdote to illustrate the importance of recording your interviews: In the late 1970s Ardeth G. Kapp, another relative on my Dutch side, scheduled a time to meet with my grandmother, Grace Berkenpas Peterson. Like Aunt Grace, Grandma Peterson had a great memory and she was closely acquainted with the first-generation immigrants in the extended family, so Ardeth wanted to interview her.

I'm sure this interview generated a valuable collection of stories, facts and information, but we don't actually know what my grandmother shared that day. Ardeth arrived well-prepared for the interview, tape recorder in hand, but the device malfunctioned, and the recording of the conversation was lost. My grandmother passed away shortly thereafter so Ardeth never had the opportunity for a second interview.

Because of Ardeth's experience with the tape recorder, and maybe because I'm a bit paranoid, I always use two separate recorders when I interview a relative (usually my smartphone and a small digital recorder). On a few occasions one of those two recording devices has failed to properly capture the entire conversation due to muffled sound, a low battery or a technical glitch, so I was especially grateful that I had the second recorder running in those instances.

While the presence of a recorder may make some people a bit nervous at the outset, they typically forget about it within a few minutes. I've never found that a recorder detracted from the quality of an interview. I have had a few situations where somebody asked that I not record a certain story or memory of a sensitive nature, and of course I honor those requests.

Modern digital recorders and smartphones have excellent microphones so you can usually pick up conversations quite clearly if you place the recorder on a table anywhere within four or five feet of where the interviewee is seated. It is also a good idea to test your recording device from different distances at home before doing the interview.

If you find that your recording was captured but the volume is very low, don't worry. It is easy to use software to amplify the volume after the fact. You can find tips on how to do this on the TechSmart Innovation YouTube channel that is listed at the end of the book.

TIP 3: Prepare Interview Questions in Advance

Before you meet with an elderly relative, it is important to prepare a list of questions in advance. You should make a list of all the information that you would like to get from the person you're meeting with, then organize that list in order of priority. Be aware that your very first question might generate a 30-minute conversation, so try to cover the most important items first. However, don't feel rushed. You can always return for a subsequent visit to cover additional items on your list that you didn't get to during the first interview.

TIP 4: Don't Interrupt

It is common for an elderly relative to suddenly remember and share other memories that are unrelated to the original topic you asked them about. I've found that these meandering conversations frequently generate the most interesting anecdotes and memories, so I've learned to never interrupt, even if the person wanders well off topic. Don't worry about time constraints or covering every single item on your list of prepared questions. As noted earlier, if you run out of time you can return for a follow-up interview to cover the remaining questions and topics.

TIP 5: How to Get in the Door

You will likely find that at least some of the people you contact will be hesitant to meet with you, especially if you don't know them. As I began scheduling meetings with my elderly relatives, I quickly exhausted the list of people whom I personally knew. I then had to begin cold-calling people and they were often confused or even suspicious as to who I was and why I wanted to talk with them. Fortunately, most of my extended family knew my grandmother well, so I always introduced myself as the grandson of Grace Berkenpas Peterson, which usually helped to ease some of the concerns or confusion.

In addition, I found that if I had something to share that was of interest to them, I had a much better chance of meeting with them. As I began to gather a collection of photos of my ancestors, this became an easy way to break the ice. I would explain to them that I had some old pictures of their mother or father or grandparents who had long since passed, and that usually got their interest. I also had many photos where I couldn't identify all of the people in them. I would sometimes ask these elderly relatives if I could stop by and show them some of my pictures and perhaps they could help to identify the ancestors in the photos.

Writing letters can also be a very effective way to contact your elderly relatives. Given the endless stream of telemarketers and robo-calls, many people, both old and young alike, are suspicious of any phone call from a person they don't know. I've found that sending a letter is sometimes a more effective method than calling, especially with relatives in their 80s or 90s. Remember, letters were a primary means of communication throughout much of their lives. A letter also gives you the opportunity to concisely explain your purpose and any information you have to share with them such as old photos, stories or a book about the family. I always include my address, phone number and email address in the letter so they can choose how they wish to respond to me.

After completing my first book about my Dutch ancestors, that publication became *by far* my most effective method for approaching people. I frequently mailed them a copy of the book in advance. Once they received the book and saw what it included, they were happy or even excited to meet with me and share their memories.

TIP 6: Photos Often Trigger Memories

Photographs are a wonderful tool in facilitating these conversations. In my very first attempt at interviewing a relative, I met with my oldest living uncle. He was known for being acquainted with a lot of people in the family, so I began with him. When I asked him if I could stop by his house to learn more about the ancestors, he agreed to meet, but he warned me that he didn't remember things as well as he used to, so he wasn't sure how much help he would be.

When I arrived at his home, I didn't begin by asking him questions. Instead, I asked him to show me his old pictures of the family. This worked beautifully. As he pulled out the old pictures, they triggered his memories of the people in the photos. He would say, "Oh, you know who this is?" and then tell me all about the various people in the picture. The photographs were a perfect catalyst for bringing back his memories from decades earlier.

I have met with a few people who have been diagnosed with early stage dementia. Even in those cases I found that photographs helped to spur memories. I have been told by some family members that people with dementia often lose their short-term memory first, so their long-term memory may still be intact and even surprisingly clear once they begin sharing old memories and stories.

TIP 7: Do Your Homework Before the Interview

Another important item to do before you conduct an interview is to research the life of the person you're meeting with. The more you understand about your interviewees' lives, including the common ancestors or relatives that they would have known personally, the better your interview will be. Make yourself aware of key events from their lives or the lives of your common ancestors.

It is also helpful to do some research into the places they lived and worked and where they attended school and church. The more you understand about your relatives' lives, the better your questions will be and the more meaningful and productive your interviews will be.

With some relatives, you will find that it is impossible to cover every topic you would like in the first meeting. I often listen to the recording of an interview and realize that I should have asked about other people or events. As noted earlier, don't hesitate to go back and meet with them again and make it an ongoing conversation.

I've formed some wonderful friendships with many of my elderly relatives through these interviews, so I now stop by to visit them whenever I'm in town, even if I don't have questions to ask. The friendships I've formed with these dear people are some of the greatest blessings I've received from doing family history work.

TIP 8: Find Out What Records They Have

One question that I always ask once I've established a comfortable conversation with a relative is if they have any family records or old photographs. If they don't, I always ask if others in their immediate family have any. My objective here is twofold.

First, I would obviously like to get access to as many records as possible. Second, I would also like to know what will happen to those records when the person who has them passes away, to ensure that the records aren't eventually lost.

One of the great tragedies I have encountered in my research was that of a great-uncle. He spent decades of his life compiling a seven-volume history of his life and his ancestors. The volumes were bound in beautiful leather books and were left to his daughter when he passed away. In the daughter's later years, the records were apparently given to another person in the family who perhaps didn't recognize their value. After an unexpected death, family members cleaned out the home and these beautiful volumes of his family's history were thrown out and lost forever.

You will find that most people are very protective of their old family photographs, and for obvious reasons. Given that sensitivity, this is a subject that I always clarify up-front. When I ask if they have old photographs, I make it clear that I would just like to take pictures of those photographs, and I do not wish to borrow or even touch the actual photos, if that's a concern. In my own family there are multiple examples of somebody borrowing priceless photographs and then misplacing or losing them, and unfortunately that scenario is not unique to my family.

As you talk to more people in your family and hopefully produce a book, a website or other documentation of your family's history, you may become the de-facto genealogist in your extended family. If that description fits you, you will likely find that people will begin offering to share information or records with you that you didn't even ask for. That can be a tremendous benefit to your research efforts.

TIP 9: Family Reunions as a Research and Networking Tool

You may be one of the fortunate people who belongs to a family that has regular reunions where elderly members of the family attend. If you are, take advantage of those occasions. While a reunion may not be an ideal time to have an in-depth sit-down interview with a relative, it is a great time to make arrangements for such a meeting. Reunions will likely be your best networking opportunity, so don't miss out on the chance to meet relatives and to get their contact information. We always pass around a note pad where everyone writes down their names, phone numbers and email addresses. I then take a photo of the note pad with my phone to ensure I have a copy. Having a photo also makes it easy to share the list with others.

If your family doesn't have regular reunions, schedule them yourself! Reunions are also a great place for people to bring photographs, stories, documents and even videos to share with others in the family. I always seem to leave my family reunions with a new collection of photos on my phone and paper records in my hand.

TIP 10: Archiving, Storing and Preserving Records

As you get to know your elderly relatives and begin compiling your family's history, people in the family may offer to give you original records in hopes that those records will be kept and stored safely and not lost. I won't cover record preservation in any detail in this book, but there are many online resources available regarding that topic.

My short suggestion would be to gladly accept these records, then make sure they are safely and properly stored. First, you should store your records in a secure location (inside your home is fine). If you have electronic records, make sure you have at least two back-up copies including one of those in a different geographic location or in the cloud (Google Drive, DropBox, or a similar cloud service). That will help to ensure that your records will never be lost. It only takes a few minutes or seconds to perform back-ups of your electronic files. My back-up copies of my electronic records saved me a few years ago when the hard drive on my home computer crashed.

If you have a collection of hard copy records, be sure to avoid storing them where they might be exposed to humidity or extreme temperatures. I also strongly recommend that any valuable or important hard copy records be scanned or photographed and "stored" electronically as an insurance policy.

LESSON 2

PUBLISH YOUR WORK

While publishing may not be part of your initial family history plan, I have learned that publishing your work is likely the best way to share and preserve the history of your family. Publishing a book obviously makes it easier to share your family's story with others, but many fail to recognize that publishing your family's story also helps to ensure that the story is not lost or forgotten in future decades.

Before you attempt to publish anything, I strongly recommend that you thoroughly research the family as your first step. That research should include the life stories of the various ancestors in question. It may also be interesting to learn about the places they lived and the important local and world events that happened during their lifetimes.

Most research can be conducted very efficiently online, making this the best time in the history of the world to do this work. I am quite familiar with the old methods that two of my grandparents used in researching our family history because I had a front-row seat to their efforts. I vividly recall tables in their homes covered with stacks of pedigree charts and other records, both printed and hand-written. It was tedious, slow, time-consuming work.

Through the benefit of online resources, we are now able

to accomplish more research in a single day than our parents or grandparents could do in weeks, months or even years. Be grateful that you're able to do your genealogy research in the age of online records!

TIP 11: Define the Scope of Your Planned Publication

At the outset of a publishing project, it is important to define the scope of your work and the type of publication you plan to produce. Are you looking to simply share a few stories and photographs? If yes, a website, a Facebook page or a small pamphlet may be the best means to accomplish this. If you're looking to document your family's story in more detail, I highly recommend publishing a book.

When I began my own research in earnest, my intent was to gather some photographs and stories about my Dutch great-great-grandparents who came to America in 1907. I never intended it to be more than 20 or 30 pages long. I just wanted a high-level story of their lives that explained their reasons for coming to the United States.

As I got deeper into my research, I realized that their story was far more interesting and important than I ever imagined. I then felt compelled to properly research, document and tell their story in a book so it would not be lost.

TIP 12: Thorough Research Makes Writing and Publishing Much Easier

I have published five books and I'm currently working on a few more. I've always found that the time spent *writing* the book accounts for a small fraction of the overall time investment. If you do your research properly, the process of putting the story into words should be relatively quick and easy, especially with some of the technology tools available today. One of the most powerful tools in this area is dictation software, which I will cover in Chapter 8.

As noted previously, one of the benefits of publishing your family story is preserving the information for future generations. There are countless examples of people who invested the time to publish a family history book but had just one copy or a few copies printed. Sadly, in many cases, those few copies of their books were then lost through carelessness, neglect or other circumstances in later years.

If you follow the publishing process that I will outline later in this chapter, I can confidently assure you that there will be a permanent archive of your family story available for future generations.

TIP 13: Don't Underestimate the Interest in Your Family's Story

One unexpected benefit of publishing a book about my family's history was the opportunity it provided me to share the story with people throughout the world. My initial goal was to document the story and make sure it was preserved in a format that people could easily read and enjoy.

My plans were not ambitious. I honestly expected that my mother and a few of my aunts and uncles would have an interest in reading the book, but I felt compelled to complete it out of respect for my great-great-grandparents and the many sacrifices they made, even if nobody read it.

What I experienced was far beyond my expectations. There was a tremendous interest in the book! Even though that interest was concentrated among members of my extended family, it was still enough for the book to be the #2 seller in its Amazon category the month it was published.

If you follow the publishing process that I outline, copies

of your book can be ordered by virtually anybody in the world with just a few clicks, and for a very reasonable cost.

Your published work will open new avenues for your research into your family's story. In my case, it has opened many doors and put me in contact with dozens if not hundreds of relatives that I never would have met otherwise.

Within six months of publishing my family history book I had sold several hundred copies through Amazon while hundreds of additional copies were made available through other distribution channels.

I never expected this sort of interest, but I don't believe my book is unique in that regard. Based on what I've found in helping others research their family histories, I think every family has a compelling story. There are likely hundreds of people in your extended family who would be interested in reading and understanding that story if it is properly told and made available to them.

The $11 selling price was a factor in the brisk sales of my book, I'm sure. Many people contacted me before it was published to ask how much the book would cost so they could determine how many copies they could afford to buy. They expected a $40 or $50 price based on other genealogy books they had seen with similar page counts. Upon seeing my book one relative said, "It's the size of a phone book!" Indeed, it is, but because self-publishing and on-demand printing (covered next in Tip 14) are so inexpensive, I was able to offer it for only $11.

I should also note that my goal was not to make money from the book, so I priced it as low as possible, just enough to cover the printing costs and the required Amazon commission fee. However, even if you wish to price your book higher and make a few dollars per copy, you can still sell your self-published book for a very reasonable price.

TIP 14: Utilize On-Demand Printing and Self-Publishing

The combination of on-demand printing and self-publishing has revolutionized the book publishing industry as a whole. If you check the latest list of top-selling works on Amazon, you will likely find that more than half of the authors on that list are self-published.

For hundreds of years, it was only cost-effective for an author to print books in quantities of thousands or even tens of thousands. On-demand printing utilizes new technology that allows a printer to print individual copies of a book, even one at a time, and still do so profitably.

Publishing genealogy books is certainly not new. Books about families and their genealogical histories have been published for centuries. I have many such books in my own collection. However, publishing those books was typically very time-consuming, expensive and cumbersome, which limited the number of works published as well as the reach and impact of those publications.

The combination of on-demand printing and self-publishing has dramatically reduced the costs and the time required to prepare a book for publication. It has also allowed many authors to publish works that never could have been published using traditional printing methods.

If you are interested in learning more about the detailed step-by-step process of utilizing self-publishing and on-demand printing for a genealogy book, you can find more information on the website www.TechSmartInnovation.com under the "Training" header.

If you would rather not go through the process of learning to do everything yourself, we also offer on-demand printing and self-publishing services for a very reasonable cost (under the "Publishing" header on the website).

The time investment to publish a book is substantial, especially for your first book. But don't let that stop you. We can assist you in making that process much faster and easier through the services and resources on our website and YouTube channel.

In my personal case, the benefits of the book have far outweighed the time investment. It's also worth noting that if I hadn't published a book, I still would have spent those same hours doing some other sort of family history research. By spending that time on the book instead of something else, I now have something tangible and long-lasting to show for those hours I invested.

My grandfather and some other family members have published books through traditional methods, and they spent tens of thousands of dollars to get their works into print. By comparison, my total cost for publishing my most recent family history book (which is 8 ½" x 11" and includes 434 pages) was just over $100!

TIP 15: Consider E-Books

A self-published book through a publisher like Amazon also offers you the ability to produce an e-book or Kindle version with very little additional effort and no additional cost. This is another benefit of self-publishing. However, I have found that the Kindle or e-book format is often not ideal for family history books, mainly because the smaller page size is not as good for displaying photographs. A hard copy book is usually the best format for publications which include a lot of photos or documents.

TIP 16: Use Your Published Book to Further Your Work

One of the great benefits of my first family history book has been the ability to give people free copies as a way to introduce myself and to give them an example of what I'm hoping to accomplish with my family history research. I have sent dozens of free copies of the book to various relatives over the past few years. As noted earlier, they are always much more interested in meeting with me to share photos, stories or other information about the family after receiving the book. The book has been the perfect icebreaker for contacting relatives whom I've never met.

I noted earlier that I've worked in the technology industry for 20+ years. As you'd expect, I'm a devout user and advocate of technology solutions. However, even though it goes against my tech instincts, I have come to believe that a hardcopy book is the ideal medium for publishing a work about your family history, even better than a Kindle or e-book version.

As noted earlier in this chapter, a hardcopy book is a much better medium for sharing and viewing old photographs. It is also a medium that can be used and enjoyed by people of all ages. While most people have computers and smartphones and are comfortable reading information on electronic devices, there are still many who prefer a hard copy book and will not read an e-book.

TIP 17: The Durability of Hardcopy Books

Looking back on the various types of computer storage media that have been used over the past 25 years, from floppy disks to CD ROM disks to SD cards and USB drives, many have gone from being widely used to largely obsolete within the span of 10 or 15 years. File formats also change from time to time, making a soft copy of a video, a story or even a photograph difficult to access or open a decade or two later.

Paper books, however, will never become obsolete. A website might become inaccessible or unpublished or the URL might change, but a hard copy book will always be something that people can read and access. There are now over 1,000 copies of my first book in the homes of my relatives throughout the world. That being the case, I'm quite comfortable that my family's story will never be completely lost or forgotten. I also have soft copies of the manuscript stored in multiple locations within my own archives, but I don't expect that to be the most effective format for archiving the book long-term.

I have been repeatedly surprised upon meeting people in other areas of the United States or even abroad who had purchased copies of my book. I didn't spend one minute or a single nickel on advertising it. My only means of promotion was informing some of my immediate family members that I was working on it and then sending out an email to let them know when it was published. Everything else happened through word of mouth. Many have found it on Amazon via Google when searching for information about my great-great-grandparents. One relative was so excited about it that she purchased 40 copies, one for each of her children and grandchildren.

In summary, self-publishing and on-demand printing allow you a very affordable, effective and simple process for turning your research into a book that can then be shared with relatives throughout the world. As the author, you can send low-priced copies of your book to anybody you wish with just a few clicks of the mouse. You can also order discounted copies directly from the publisher. The convenience and power of this innovative publishing model offers you a tremendous opportunity as a genealogist, but only if you utilize it.

You may be thinking that this all sounds great, but you're not convinced that you could publish a book by yourself. I was also intimidated by the prospect of publishing a book when I first began to consider that option, but I couldn't believe how simple and easy the process was. I am comfortable in saying that anybody who can do basic family history work can also publish a book after some basic instruction or assistance.

Again, if you're looking for more information about self-publishing or if you would like to take a class on how to turn your family history records and information into a book, visit the website www.TechSmartInnovation.com for more information.

LESSON 3

HIDDEN TREASURES IN COMMUNITY RECORDS

The topics covered in Lesson 3 comprise an especially broad category of family history record sources. This chapter could easily include many additional community record types, but I will focus on just four which I have found to be especially useful and productive in my research: Newspapers, School Yearbooks, City Directories, and Cemeteries.

Newspapers

Early in my research, I found links to some old newspaper articles available online which appeared to contain information about my ancestors. However, I couldn't access the articles without purchasing a subscription to the website where they were located.

As I expanded my research efforts, I found a few free online newspaper archives, but most of what I wanted was still not available without a subscription. Being cheap, I didn't want to pay for a subscription that I might not use enough to justify the purchase. So, I held off and instead made a list of the newspaper articles I wanted to access, hoping that they might become available free of charge in the future.

After a year or so, I finally broke down and paid for the subscription, and no money I have spent on family history work was probably better spent. Newspapers are a tremendous source of information, and my collection of documents now includes over 3,500 articles from a single newspaper, with thousands more from other papers.

Newspapers.com has the largest collection of searchable newspapers available. If you are going to use a single source to begin your search of newspapers, you should start there. Be sure to check out the TechSmart Innovation YouTube channel for step-by-step videos for Tips 18, 19, 20 and 21.

TIP 18: Search for Street Addresses

While your initial search for your ancestors will be for their actual names, you'll find that names are often misspelled in newspaper articles. However, you can still find what you are seeking, even if their names aren't spelled correctly.

One feature of most old newspaper articles is that any mention of a member of the community was typically followed by his or her street address. By searching for the street addresses of my ancestors (i.e., "123 Jefferson St") instead of their names, I significantly increased the number of articles I found about my ancestors.

As you would expect, the names of immigrants are especially susceptible to being misspelled. Fortunately, street names in a city or town are well-known to reporters, so you rarely miss a result if you're searching for the street address.

TIP 19: Search for Alternate Spellings or Misspellings

By searching for street addresses, I also noticed some common misspellings of my ancestors' names (i.e., Smith instead of Smit). I also found alternate spellings (often "Americanized" versions of their names) that some in the family used. If I see the same misspelling or alternate spelling more than once, I also search newspapers.com for that spelling of the name and I typically find additional results.

I have been amazed at the number of times some names were misspelled in print. One of my ancestors, Uuldrik Kap, had his first name spelled 12 different ways in newspaper articles and public records. His last name was also spelled several different ways, so I always recommend that you search for as many variations as you can come up with. If your ancestor's given name is Jon or Jan, try searching for John as well. If the surname is Johansson or Johanssen, try searching for similar names like Johnson or Jansen or even Jensen.

TIP 20: Search for Your Ancestor's Hometown or Home Country

If you are looking for information about ancestors who came from a foreign country, it may also be useful to search newspapers.com for their hometown, home province or even their home country along with their name in a combined search. If your ancestor came from an obscure town or a small country, such searches can be especially productive.

Most of my Dutch ancestors came from a rural province in the Netherlands called Groningen. While their names were almost always spelled incorrectly, the province name was usually spelled properly. By searching for the province name of Groningen, I found many references to my ancestors and members of their extended families that I didn't find by searching for their names.

By searching for the province, I also found connections between my ancestors and other immigrants from the same area, since their names were frequently mentioned together in articles about anniversary parties, birthday parties or funerals. This helped me discover some close relationships between my Dutch ancestors and others from Groningen where there had been no obvious connection before my search. In many cases I then asked my elderly relatives if they were close to these families and they confirmed some important connections and relationships.

TIP 21: Why Can't I Find My Female Ancestors?

Up until at least the mid-20th-century, most references to women in local newspapers referred to them as Mrs. John Doe (i.e., by their husband's name), excluding the woman's first name from the reference. You may find that searches for your grandmothers or great-grandmothers are not particularly productive, but that will change if you begin searching for their husband's name preceded by "Mrs." If your grandmother was Mary Smith and her husband was John, try searching for "Mrs. John Smith" instead of "Mary Smith" and you will significantly improve your search results.

TIP 22: Other Online Newspaper Sources

I already mentioned my subscription to newspapers.com, which has been extremely useful. Ancestry.com now owns newspapers.com, so many of the newspapers.com results are included with an ancestry.com subscription. There are also several other repositories of newspapers online, including:

- http://digitalnewspapers.org
- http://chroniclingamerica.loc.gov/

A Google search for "online newspaper archives" will also give you additional results. In addition, most current newspapers have a searchable archive available on their websites, but the time frame is usually limited to recent years.

TIP 23: Still More Newspaper Archives

City and county libraries often have archives of local newspapers in their collections, including many on microfilm or microfiche. If you are unable to find what you are looking for online or on the newspaper's current website, you should visit the libraries in the town or city where your ancestors lived and search the newspaper archives there.

School Yearbooks

Like newspapers, school yearbooks have been a very valuable resource in my research efforts. If you happen to have an ancestor's school yearbook this can be especially interesting. Such a yearbook not only has photos and information about your ancestor, it may also include personal notes written to him or her by classmates.

TIP 24: Start with the Ancestry.com Collection

While the collection is nowhere near complete, ancestry.com has many school yearbooks scanned and searchable in its online archives. The ancestry.com archive continues to grow over time, and it is fully indexed, which makes it very easy to find the people you're searching for (if ancestry.com has the yearbooks you want in their collection). There are other options for finding yearbooks as I will explain shortly, but those will probably require a greater investment of time than simply searching the ancestry.com collection.

TIP 25: Go Directly to the Source

If you are unable to find the yearbooks for your ancestors on ancestry.com or another online source, I highly recommend going directly to the source by accessing the archives at the high schools which your ancestors attended.

Most of my ancestors who settled in my hometown of Ogden, Utah attended one of the two major local high schools. My search of the online copies of those yearbooks yielded some useful results but didn't include most of the years I was looking for. So, I went to the high school libraries to see original copies of the yearbooks. Every high school library I have checked has an archive of old yearbooks.

The first time I did this, I contacted the school librarian and asked if I could visit the school and view the old yearbooks. She was happy to facilitate my request. She explained the best days and times to do this and I arrived with my laptop and my smartphone. In the end, my smartphone was all I needed. I photographed the yearbooks two pages at a time, and it took five or six hours to photograph a set of yearbooks covering a 30-year period.

I followed the same process with the other high school in Ogden. This collection was larger, so I brought my young daughter with me and she helped by turning and holding the pages as I photographed them. Her help made the process very quick. We were able to photograph nearly 40 years of yearbooks in a few hours.

As a side note, my daughter really enjoyed the opportunity to visit the high school where her grandmother and other ancestors had attended school decades earlier. The school in question (Ogden High School) is also a beautiful historic building and that added to the experience. It is never too early to start sharing some of your interesting family history experiences with your children or grandchildren. If they develop an interest, they will likely continue the work when you are gone.

TIP 26: How to Make the Photographed Yearbooks Searchable

After photographing all of these yearbooks, I had more than 4,000 images on my phone which I then transferred to my computer. However, searching through those 4,000 photographs for my ancestors' names and photos, page by page, was tedious and very inefficient, so I applied technology to develop a much faster solution.

Using Adobe Acrobat, I was able to convert each set of photographs into a digital PDF file for each yearbook. This process took a minute or two for each year. Once the PDF files were complete, I then used the optical character recognition (OCR) capabilities in Adobe to convert the text in the PDF yearbooks into actual searchable text. The conversion was very accurate, and it worked perfectly as long as my photographs were reasonably well-focused.

Once the file conversions were complete, which again took a few minutes each, I was able to search these new "digital yearbooks" for my ancestors' names in a matter of seconds, saving me a total of fifty hours or more. Refer to my YouTube video for Tip 26 for a step-by-step overview of how to do this.

City Directories

TIP 27: Find Occupation, Employer, Spouse and Other Information

City directories are another online resource which includes a wonderful collection of information about your ancestors. Ancestry.com and other websites offer extensive collections of city directories for most major cities and even many smaller cities and towns, going back as far as the late 19th century.

For most of the 20th century, directory listings included the expected fields of name and address, just as you would find in a recent directory listing. However, these older directories also typically included spouse, employer, occupation and whether a person was a boarder or a student that year.

Directories used a variety of abbreviations to denote some of this information, including given names and occupations, so be sure to check out the abbreviation translation page in the front of each directory as you review your results.

As with newspapers, there are often misspellings in city directories, so searching these directories for the street address in addition to the ancestor's name will yield a much more complete list of results for your ancestors. Searching for common misspellings or spelling variations of your ancestors' names will also improve your results.

TIP 28: Create a Directory Spreadsheet for Your Ancestors

As I searched through city directories covering an 80-year period, I recorded some of my key findings in a spreadsheet so I wouldn't have to go back and find the information again. I figured this would save me a little time, but I have referred to these spreadsheets hundreds of times since. They have become an invaluable resource in my research efforts, putting important information that I frequently reference at my fingertips, all accessible with just a few clicks in a matter of seconds.

These spreadsheets have also allowed me to identify many

instances where my ancestors were neighbors or even lived in the same residence, offering another unique peek into their lives and close relationships. I never would have found these without having the directory information in a spreadsheet where it could be quickly searched, sorted and filtered.

When I interviewed one relative, Edna, who was in her 90s, I asked about her cousin, Bernice. My spreadsheet indicated that Bernice had lived near Edna when they were children. I also knew from my research that Edna had a total of 68 cousins on her father's side alone, so asking about specific cousins was not necessarily near the top of my "to-do" list. But I asked her about Bernice because of what the spreadsheet information showed, and it paid off.

Edna confirmed that she and Bernice were indeed neighbors when they were young. She then shared several wonderful stories about her close friendship with Bernice. Edna and Bernice remained very close until Bernice's passing at age 92. Without my spreadsheet, I would not have known to ask about that connection and I would have missed out on a particularly interesting family connection. Edna also put me in contact with Bernice, so my address spreadsheet also yielded a new research contact for my work.

TIP 29: City Directories from England and Wales

Since a large percentage of Americans have at least some English ancestry, the collection of local and trade directories offered by the University of Leicester is a great resource. The collection spans both England and Wales from the 1760s until the 1910s, offering an excellent information source to identify where your English or Welsh ancestors lived. This can be especially useful if you plan to visit your ancestral homeland in England or Wales. The collection can be accessed by searching on Google for "historical directories of England and Wales, Leicester."

The collection is extensive, with hundreds of indexed directories which are fully searchable. Simply select the region you wish to search, select a directory, and begin searching!

Cemeteries

Cemeteries are perhaps the oldest and most widely-used source of information for genealogy researchers. Websites like findagrave.com and billiongraves.com are very popular online resources for both experienced and amateur family history researchers, and for good reason. These websites are extremely useful and efficient and can save you a lot of time, giving you access to cemeteries around the world from the convenience of your computer.

However, online cemetery databases are far from complete and they may contain inaccuracies due to the human element of photographing and transcribing very old and often hard-to-read inscriptions. For this reason, your research of cemetery records should include a visit to the actual cemetery if at all possible, especially if you have multiple ancestors buried at a given cemetery.

TIP 30: Create a Cemetery Information Spreadsheet

I always like to add the burial information I find online to a simple spreadsheet, just as I do with the city directory information. Again, this allows you to search and filter the names by cemetery or even by section of the cemetery, making your visits much more productive.

Many cemetery websites have interactive maps showing the geographic location of burial plots, including the GPS coordinates in some cases. By mapping these out before you go, you can make your visit much more efficient and enjoyable. My YouTube tips include more detail on this one.

TIP 31: Prepare a List and a Map

Before visiting a cemetery, use the information spreadsheet from Tip 30 to create a list of the graves you want to visit at that location. If you sort the spreadsheet by burial plot location (refer to my YouTube video for Tip 31 for an example of how to do this) you can then search the cemetery by section and find the grave locations much more quickly.

If you don't know the name or location of the cemetery where your ancestor is buried, you can almost always find that information through findagrave.com, billiongraves.com, familysearch.org or through obituaries or funeral announcements published in old newspapers.

TIP 32: Try the Interactive App from Billiongraves.com

Billiongraves.com has an app with an interactive map that is very impressive. The app works extremely well as long as your ancestor's grave is in their database and you have a cell phone signal at the cemetery. I have found a few cases where my ancestor's name was not yet in the database and I had spotty cell service in a couple of cemetery locations, but it is a really impressive tool that is definitely worth exploring. More cemeteries are being photographed and added to their database all the time, and cell coverage continues to improve, so this app will become increasingly useful over time. If you haven't tried this one yet, you need to.

TIP 33: Stop by the Cemetery Office During Your Visit

One other valuable resource that many people fail to utilize is the cemetery office. I always stop at the office of a cemetery (if there is one) to ask the staff if they have any information or tips to help in my search. I have always found them to be helpful, providing maps, directions and other information.

Cemeteries and mortuaries may also have funeral or burial records on file in hardcopy. These records, if available, typically include a lot of useful details about your ancestors. Visiting the cemetery or mortuary office is a great option to explore if you are struggling to find information about an ancestor and have exhausted other avenues and resources. These detailed funeral and burial records are not typically available online, so you can only find them by calling or visiting the cemetery offices.

TIP 34: Finding an Ancestor's Burial Location

One other benefit from visiting and talking with the staff at a cemetery is demonstrated with the case of Frank Kapp, one of my ancestors. Frank passed away as an infant in the 1940s, but I could not find his burial location. I had checked the online cemetery databases and walked through the local cemetery where his parents were eventually buried, but I found nothing. His living siblings had also searched for his burial location for years, but to no avail.

Having exhausted the standard search methods, I finally called the office of the Aultorest Mortuary and Cemetery in Ogden, Utah. This was not the cemetery where Frank's parents were buried, but his grandparents were buried there, so I decided to give it a shot.

I asked the person who answered my call to check to see if they had any records on file for a Frank Kapp, also instructing her to check for the alternate spelling of Kap. I was thrilled when she called me back a couple of days later to inform me that they had found Frank's burial records!

Frank had indeed been buried at the Aultorest cemetery, but in an unmarked grave, so his name didn't show up on any of the lists of grave markers. His surname was also misspelled on the official records as Kap instead of Kapp.

The woman in the office was able to give me the exact location of the unmarked grave, which I learned was right next to others in the family, including Frank's grandparents and my grandparents.

Upon receiving this information, I ordered a grave marker for Frank. His burial site is now properly marked so family members can visit his burial location, leave flowers and have a place to remember him. After decades of futile searches for his resting place, two of Frank's living brothers were elated to finally know where their younger brother was buried. This wouldn't have been possible if I hadn't contacted the cemetery office.

Grave marker for Frank Kapp at Aultorest Cemetery
in Ogden, Utah

LESSON 4

Using Online Genealogy Databases Effectively

Online genealogy databases like familysearch.org, ancestry.com, findagrave.com, billiongraves.com and fold3.com have revolutionized the way family history research is done throughout the world. A strong understanding of these powerful tools is essential in making your research as efficient, effective and comprehensive as possible.

I could easily fill multiple volumes with information about how to use these sites, but I will focus only on some basic approaches and methods along with a few tips and tricks. If you are interested in gaining a deeper understanding of these websites and how to use them, please visit the TechSmart Innovation website for a list of available training classes.

TIP 35: Should I Pay for a Subscription?

If you are very serious about your research, the subscription to a database like ancestry.com is worth every penny. Many of these subscription-based websites also offer free trials, so take advantage of that option if you aren't sure that you will use a subscription. Most also offer monthly subscriptions, so if you only need access to a specific set of records and can retrieve what you need within a fairly short period of time, go for the monthly option.

TIP 36: Use Your Time Wisely on These Sites

Efficiency is the key to effective (and enjoyable) genealogy research. Your success should not be measured by the number of hours you spend researching, but by the results of that research. If you are investing 10 hours a month or 10 hours a week, what do you have to show for that time investment?

Sources like ancestry.com contain such a wide range of records that you could spend months researching your family and still miss some of the important records unless your research approach is focused and efficient.

People frequently cite an unnamed "scientific" study indicating that people use less than 10% of their brains. I don't know who first came up with that number nor if it is accurate. However, after decades of doing computer-based research and training people to use computers more efficiently, I *am* confident in saying that the average person uses less than 10% of their home computer's capability.

To continue this theme (there is a point here), after teaching countless people to use online genealogy databases like ancestry.com and familysearch.org, I also believe the average subscriber uses less than 10% of these sites' full capabilities and offerings.

Time is often the limiting factor. Most users are barely scratching the surface of the information contained therein and are, therefore, missing many of the valuable benefits and resources.

I've seen many cases where people spent hundreds of hours to find information, records or sources that could have been found in perhaps 10 or 20 hours with a more efficient research approach. Does that describe your experience with these online databases? Are you unsure? Keeping a research log (sample below) can give you an indication of how efficient you are in your research. Are you becoming more efficient or less efficient over time? Create a spreadsheet to record the number of records you find per hour or per day and track your results over a period of months. The YouTube channel video for Tip 36 includes more details on how to do that.

An example of a standard research log

TIP 37: Using "Suggested Records" in Ancestry.com

In ancestry.com, use the "suggested records" to the right of a search result if you have confirmed that the record is indeed that of your ancestor. Checking these suggested records is a very efficient way to *quickly* search a lot of possible record matches for your ancestor's name.

The database itself is doing most of the work for you by searching, sorting and prioritizing results to determine the likelihood of a match. These suggested record hints (screenshot example below) are not always matches. In fact, they are frequently not matches, but you will find many more matching records and will find them much more efficiently by utilizing these hints than you will by running individual searches on your own. See the YouTube video for Tip 37 for an example of how to do this.

TIP 38: Hover Over Search Results - No Need to Click

If you have a list of results for a search in ancestry.com, you can hover over these records and it will give you a preview of the record details without having to click the link. For example, if you have pulled up a list of city directory results, you can hover your mouse pointer over these results and you can see the year of the directory and also confirm the address location for your ancestor without clicking the link.

This is much faster than clicking on each result and then clicking the back button after viewing each one. It may only save you 10 or 15 seconds per record, but after hundreds of records, those savings really add up. This approach is also at least 100 times faster than going to the actual city directories and scrolling through them page by page to confirm where your ancestors lived each year. The YouTube clip for Tip 38 includes a step-by-step example.

TIP 39: Utilize Message Boards & Research Communities

There are research communities and message boards on websites like ancestry.com and even Facebook which can magnify your ability to find records and answer questions quickly. These are typically popular places for experienced researchers to share ideas and offer tips. I am quite familiar with the databases of Dutch vital statistics at www.wiewaswie.nl, but I had one Dutch ancestor with a long gap in his timeline and I could find no explanation for this gap. I finally took this question to a message board on ancestry.com and within 48 hours I had the answer that had eluded me. The man who answered the question was an expert on the area where my ancestor had lived, and he was able to access other records which were not available online.

TIP 40: Census Record Results Expanded

There are many underutilized databases and research

sources within ancestry.com, and one example is with census records. While census records are one of the most widely accessed record categories on ancestry.com, one additional feature that is often missed is the "Neighbors" link, which allows you to see other people listed on the same census page as your ancestor.

By clicking on the "View others on page" link (screen shot above) you can see a list of the residents and families who lived in the same neighborhood as your ancestor, including their birthplaces, languages spoken and other useful facts.

TIP 41: "Hidden" Treasures in Original Immigration Records

Immigration records are some of the most valuable and frequently-used collections of records on sites like ancestry.com and familysearch.org. However, I have found that most people rely primarily or even exclusively on the indexed information from these archives. They do this because it is easier and faster and the handwriting is often difficult to read on the original records. While the indexed information is generally accurate and is very helpful from an initial search standpoint, it has two potential gaps.

First, the original passenger lists from immigration ships often contain other details which are not included in the indexed results. For example, I have frequently found notes in the original records showing the ticket cost, the traveler's final destination and the person(s) they planned to stay or live with at that final destination, but those details were not included in the indexed information.

Details like this offer important insights into an ancestor's immigration voyage as well as their family relationships and economic circumstances, but you miss those key insights if you don't review the actual hand-written ship manifest. Completing a course in Paleography (Tip 86) can make reading the handwriting in these records much easier.

Second, the indexed records frequently contain errors which can confuse or hamper your research. Ship manifests and passenger lists are often difficult to read and to index. This is understandable given the age of the original documents and the conditions in which ship records were kept. The prevalence of non-English names is also a contributor to the errors. In my experience, a significant percentage of my ancestors' names were misspelled on immigration records, in some cases well more than half.

I certainly don't mean to disparage or question the value of worldwide indexing efforts here. I have contributed to those efforts myself and this book highlights the great value of indexing work. However, this is one area where there are frequently challenges, so it is useful to call those out.

TIP 42: Using FamilySearch.org as a Free Alternative to Ancestry.com

FamilySearch.org has a huge collection of records in its archives, comparable in size to the collection on ancestry.com. One benefit of FamilySearch is that it does not require a paid subscription. If your focus is searching for such items as census, marriage, birth, death and other public records and you are hesitant to invest in a subscription to ancestry.com, you can find much of what you need on FamilySearch.org. The video for Tip 42 on the YouTube channel includes some examples of FamilySearch.org resources.

TIP 43: FamilySearch Users as an Information Resource

FamilySearch.org benefits from a huge and growing base of dedicated users who make millions of contributions to the site every week, adding valuable new information to an already expansive database. If you have hit a dead end on one of your ancestors and that individual is one of the 1.2 billion people listed in the FamilySearch database (as of 2019), you may find help from the site's user community.

By clicking on an ancestor's "person" page, you can see a "Latest Changes" link on the right side of the page. The three most recent changes to that person's record will be listed, along with a link to "Show All" changes.

Each change on the list will include the user name of the

FamilySearch user who made the change. If you click on the user name, you will see the contact information for that user.

I've had tremendous success in contacting and working with FamilySearch users who are actively contributing to my ancestors' records. If they have a photo, a story or a document to add for an ancestor, there is a good chance they have more than that. I have found this to be an especially effective way to find information, and many of these users were actually distant (or not-so-distant) cousins, an added bonus!

FamilySearch also includes an option to "enable relationship viewing." If you click this option, it will allow you to see your relationship (if any) to other users, assuming both users have enabled the feature. It basically adds RelativeFinder.org features to FamilySearch.org.

Visit the TechSmart Innovation YouTube channel for more details on how to use this feature. This approach of contacting users who are making contributions to an ancestor's record will also work on other sites, as highlighted in the next tip.

TIP 44: Findagrave, Billiongraves and Ancestry Users as an Information Source

I have also found many valuable records by contacting users who added comments to an ancestor's burial record on findagrave.com or billiongraves.com, or those who have created a personal pedigree for that ancestor on ancestry.com. Just click on the usernames of the people making changes. This is also covered in my YouTube video for this tip.

TIP 45: The "Watch" Feature in FamilySearch.org

FamilySearch.org also offers the ability to "watch" an ancestor by clicking a star at the top of their "person" page. This allows you to receive email notifications when anybody makes a change to the records you are watching. FamilySearch also has a "list" function under the "Family Tree" menu which allows you to see all of the ancestors you are watching. You can also click on the "changes to people I'm watching" link at the top of the list page to see all changes to the ancestors on your watch list, in sequential order. The YouTube video for Tip 45 and Tip 46 includes a step-by-step demonstration of this one.

TIP 46: Filtering the Recent Changes for your Watch List

After using this "watch" function in FamilySearch.org for several years, I now have over 300 ancestors on my watch list. I am especially interested in finding new stories or photos which are added to the ancestors I'm watching.

Filtering the FamilySearch Watch list for "photo" (Tips 45 & 46)

To quickly check to see if any new stories or photos have been added for the people on my list, I can click on the "changes to people I'm watching" link and then use the search/filter window to search for "story" or "photo." It will then show me all of the stories or photos that have been added, by ancestor, in sequential order.

Finding these new stories and photos for my ancestors is always exciting, but the contact name of the person who added them is sometimes even more valuable to my long-term research efforts.

As referenced previously, if a user has photos or stories to add for an ancestor, it is very likely that they have other information, so I frequently contact those users to see what else they may be willing to share. Not every user replies, but I've found that if I offer to send them a free copy of my book or to share some of my own research on that common ancestor, they frequently reply and share other materials of interest.

Because of the dynamic nature of these online genealogy database websites, I have not attempted to add a comprehensive list of the various functions or tools. That list would be constantly changing, and it could probably fill multiple volumes, as noted earlier. However, you can visit my YouTube channel to find my latest videos showing how sites like Ancestry, FamilySearch, Findagrave, BillionGraves and Fold3 can be used most efficiently and effectively.

Training courses are also available on our website TechSmartInnovation.com. Look under the "Training" header to find courses that offer an in-depth understanding of these tools, or of other topics covered in this book.

LESSON 5

TRAVELING TO YOUR ANCESTRAL HOMELAND

Most people with a serious interest in genealogy eventually feel a desire to visit their ancestral homeland(s), to walk the streets where their forebears walked and to see the places where they lived. My Grandpa Parkinson traveled to Bolton, England in the 1980s and had a marvelous experience which included finding obscure Church of England records that he could not have found without traveling to Bolton.

However, I know others who traveled to their family homelands and saw the cities where their ancestors lived and had a fun tourist experience, but they came up empty in terms of family history findings. Such trips can be very disappointing to a family history enthusiast. In my experience, a less-than-fulfilling trip to the homeland is often due to a lack of preparation for that trip beforehand.

Meeting Heber and Ardeth G. Kapp was one of the blessings of my research into my ancestors. Ardeth is widely recognized as an educator, author and church leader, but she is also an extraordinary organizer. At one of our first family reunions (which Ardeth and I organized together), she asked if I would be willing to take a group to the Netherlands if there were people interested. I agreed to do so, thinking that maybe five or six people would sign up.

To my great surprise, when I asked who might be interested in traveling to the Netherlands, more than 40 people expressed a serious interest! I decided at that point that I would require people to sign up and make a down payment on their flights six months in advance to make sure they were serious. Again, much to my surprise, 30 people signed up and paid their money! Our trip was on, and what an adventure it was!

We had an incredible experience in the Netherlands. Janice Kapp Perry, one of the relatives who joined us on the trip, wrote a beautiful summary of our experiences there. I've included a few excerpts, with her permission:

"<u>Monday</u>: I was sitting by the window seat as we were coming into Holland and the lush green fields and orderly look of the country just overwhelmed me and tears came quite unexpectedly. For almost a lifetime I wanted to see Holland and here I am!

"<u>Saturday</u>: "We toured up and down the streets of Hellum and Siddeburen where some of our ancestors attended church. The homes are so distinctively Dutch and are kept so clean and decorative. As soon as we got to Groningen and Siddeburen I felt such a change in our trip, like the Spirit entered into us in a palpable way. I could hardly believe I was in the very spot where they lived and were first taught the gospel and suffered 18 years of persecution before they could start migrating to Zion. I hoped they were aware of our pilgrimage to their homeland.

"We travelled on briefly to a spot where we could see Germany across the water! After that it was time to drive to the church in Groningen where the members had prepared a grand welcome for us! They were out in the parking lot grilling every kind of meat you could name, and it was a joyous time greeting them and feeling their great spirit. Best part of the trip!

"We enjoyed the meal together (and what a spread it was!) and then groups were all over the hall visiting animatedly trying to make connections with relatives. It was one happy beehive of excited people, and we just marveled at all that was going on. I sat in the chapel for a few minutes and said a heartfelt prayer of thanks for being here and just felt overwhelmed with a feeling of 'coming home.' It seems like a dream.

"Sunday: It has been fun to meet cousins and second cousins, etc. who I didn't grow up with because we moved from Ogden when I was eight. They're all such nice friends to share a trip with. Amsterdam was extremely interesting and quite challenging trying to avoid being hit by bicycles, cars or buses going fast in very narrow lanes and paths. One could spend a long time here seeing the sights. I think we chose well and saw the right things."

- Janice Kapp Perry

There are several keys to making a trip to your ancestral homeland useful and productive. While every country is different and will require unique accommodations and preparation, these tips should be of use in any European country you visit. They should also be useful in many other countries around the world based on my experience in traveling to Latin America and Asia.

TIP 47: Know What You're Looking For

You should research your family's history *in* the ancestral homeland as much as possible before you go. Use available records to find out where they lived, where they worked and where they went to church. Research both your direct line ancestors and extended family who lived in the area you are visiting. Census records, birth records, marriage records and other sources will give you insights into the places where these important events took place. With that knowledge in hand, you can then focus a portion or all of your trip on visiting, seeing and experiencing the very places where your ancestors lived.

TIP 48: Prepare an Itinerary

Traveling in a foreign country, especially if you haven't previously visited it, can be a confusing and frustrating experience. The best way to avoid unnecessary confusions, frustrations and wasted time is to prepare a detailed yet flexible itinerary before your trip. Your itinerary should include the places you plan to visit, the day/time you will visit those places and the transportation methods you plan to use.

I strongly recommend planning generous time estimates for each key stop on the trip. This will allow you the flexibility to spend more time in a place if you find it to be of particular interest. I also recommend buying any tickets in advance whenever possible. That would include transportation tickets or entrance fees for attractions such as museums, tours, or anything else. Paying in advance will expedite the process and allow you to avoid any unnecessary challenges with currency exchange or credit cards.

The concierge at your hotel can also be helpful in arranging for transportation or visits to key tourist attractions. If you are renting a car, make sure you also verify or arrange for parking in advance, as that is not always an easy arrangement to make in European countries.

TIP 49: Traveling in a Group Can Be Especially Fun and Effective

Traveling with a group of relatives is fun and it can also add to the effectiveness of your trip. During our time in Amsterdam in 2017, there were so many places to visit and not everybody wanted to do the same thing, so we were able to split our large group into three or four smaller groups each day to give everyone a chance to visit the places and attractions they wanted to see.

While a large group does make the planning and logistics more complex, we solved much of that (including flights and hotel reservations) by using a travel agency. As we traveled from Amsterdam to the small villages of Groningen where our ancestors had lived, we utilized a motor coach with a professional driver. The driver shared interesting insights along the way and somehow managed to steer a huge bus through some very narrow countryside roads.

The tour bus ride was especially fun. Jan Weening, my friend from Groningen who is also an expert on the history of the area, agreed to be our tour guide. He prepared and printed handouts for each of us. The handouts were extremely useful in helping everyone understand where we were going and how each of these places was connected to our family's ancestry. While most of us were not acquainted prior to the trip, we soon became close friends. The group felt like one big family after spending a week together.

I also invited a few of our local Dutch relatives (whom I had met on my previous trips to the Netherlands) to join us in the tour bus during the four days we spent in Groningen. This gave us another wonderful opportunity to spend precious time with our distant cousins. They shared their own memories and stories about our common ancestors and the various places we visited together. This added a delightful local flavor to the visit.

TIP 50: Mode of Transportation Options

Renting a car or taking Ubers or taxis seems to work best for traveling in places like Europe, especially in rural areas. I always prefer a car or taxi to taking trains or buses because the car allows you the flexibility of changing your route on the fly. It also includes the benefit of seeing the small towns and villages along your path. There may be portions of your trip where a train or bus is the best option, but the flexibility of a car has been great in my experience.

If you are traveling with a group of 10 or more people, I highly recommend chartering a motor coach or tour bus. As noted earlier, we used this method for our 30-person tour group, and it was perfect. The cost was also surprisingly affordable. The motor coach was comfortable, the driver was entertaining and knowledgeable, and the hours together on the bus allowed us to get to know one another better and to discuss information and stories about our ancestors.

TIP 51: Do I Need a Tour Guide?

A tour guide is certainly not necessary, but having a local expert can be very helpful. I'm sure that our time in Holland would have still been enjoyable and interesting, even without Jan Weening's help as our tour guide, but it would have been much less productive and informative. His contributions to our trip included:

- Preparing and printing handouts with information about each place we visited
- Making connections and arrangements to meet with local historians and local family members

- Arranging a formal reception where a local government official welcomed us to the municipality of Slochteren
- Reserving a hall at the local church building for a family reception with our local Dutch relatives
- Coordinating the catering and preparation for that reception
- Sharing interesting facts about the area as we drove from site to site in the motor coach
- Translating for us with the local contacts who didn't speak English. While most people speak English in Amsterdam and the other big cities, it was more common to find people who spoke only Dutch, including some of the local Dutch dialects, in Groningen.

TIP 52: Making Connections Through Local Newspapers

Perhaps the most powerful method we used in finding living relatives and other information in our ancestral homeland was accomplished through the small-town local newspapers. Jan Weening suggested posting notices in the local papers a few weeks prior to our large group arriving. In these articles he explained that 30 members of the Kap and Boekweg families would be visiting the villages in the Slochteren, Groningen area.

These newspaper articles asked that any descendants of Antje Kap or Harmina Boekweg contact us, because we were very interested in meeting with them during our visit. Antje and Harmina, two of our ancestors, gave us a unique connection to the area. When our Kap and Boekweg ancestors came to America between 1899 and 1907, these two cousins of my great-grandmother remained in Holland. They later married and had children in Holland, while their parents, siblings and cousins had immigrated to America. Very little was known about Antje or Harmina prior to our trip, although I had confirmed that they each had children and grandchildren.

Jan reserved the local church building so these relatives could meet with us there. His newspaper article idea worked even better than we had hoped! More than 35 relatives (all descendants of Antje or Harmina) came to meet us, including many who had traveled across the country to be there!

Groningen Historian and Tour Guide Extraordinaire, Jan Weening

The church building also had three computers with FamilySearch.org available. This allowed everyone to quickly verify our common ancestors and to see how we were all related. There were many other local relatives who responded to the newspaper articles who were not able to meet with us due to schedule conflicts, but they shared their email addresses, phone numbers, and mailing addresses which yielded even more useful information.

Tip 53: Help from Local Historians and Historical Organizations

I initially underestimated the value of local Dutch historical societies in my genealogy efforts. However, these organizations in your ancestral homeland can be of great use. For example, there is a maritime museum in the province of Groningen where I was able to find information about the members of my family who worked on ships in that area, including ship ownership records and muster rolls. The museum also had some records available online, but the records at the actual museum were much more extensive.

During my various trips to the Netherlands, I have also visited the Groningen historical society's office and archive. They have an expansive collection and were very friendly and willing to help with any research needs.

I was also able to visit the home of a local historian who had spent years compiling an extensive history of every house in Siddeburen, the town where most of my ancestors lived. His records went back more than 100 years. He had also published some beautiful hard-cover books which contained an ownership history of each home along with hundreds of color photographs. I never imagined that such specialized and detailed historical information would exist for this small town of 3,000 people. This unexpected resource was found through a simple Google search by my friend, Jan Weening.

Jan Weening's name has been mentioned extensively here, and for good reason. No other individual has given me more information, assistance or guidance in my research efforts than this good man, who has become a dear friend. He also introduced me to various books and publications which I never would have found without him. In addition, he recently published a book of his own and he presented me with a copy during my most recent trip to Groningen in November, 2019. As you might expect, the book is excellent!

When Jan and I first met, I was trying to discover the history of my ancestors before they left Holland. Meanwhile, Jan was trying to figure out what happened to the hundreds of people who left Groningen and settled in Utah, including members of his own family. Together, we have been able to combine our efforts and piece together the entire story of these families, including many shared ancestors.

Tip 54: Local Government Officials

Millions of Americans visit Amsterdam and other tourist areas of the Netherlands every year, but tour groups are rare in the small, rural towns throughout the country. Jan Weening astutely recognized this. He knew that a visit by a group of 30 Americans, all with local ancestral roots, was a unique event in that small community. So, he informed the local government officials of our group's visit, thinking that they might also find it of interest.

Jan was soon contacted by the office of Jan Jakob Boersma, the *Wethouder* or Deputy Mayor of the Slochteren municipality, who asked if our tour group would be interested in attending a formal reception to welcome us. We were of course honored to accept this generous invitation!

Mr. Boersma was hospitable and impressive. He formally welcomed us with a speech (in English) on the grounds of the Fraeylemaborg Castle. He and his office also arranged for delicious refreshments to be served and invited a newspaper reporter and a photographer to cover the event. An article describing our visit to Slochteren was published in the local paper along with a large color photograph.

Formal reception for our tour group at Fraeylemaborg Castle, 2017

Our tour group with Slochteren Deputy Mayor Jan Jakob Boersma

Mr. Boersma also introduced us to the curator of Fraeylemaborg Castle, and she shared additional historical information about the municipality where our family lived.

Tip 55: Other Local Individuals, Including Local Relatives

In addition to amateur and professional historians, you may find that you will gain the best information about your family from your distant relatives who still live in the areas where your ancestors lived.

During our 2017 Holland trip we met with a Mr. Broekema, whose family owned a farm where our ancestor Harmina Boekweg had worked for decades. He shared pictures, memories, and other records with us, providing a beautiful overview of Harmina and her life. He also put us in contact with her living grandchildren who are our distant cousins.

We also met with Hilko, a third cousin who lived in the same home where his grandmother, Antje Kap, had lived with her husband and children for many years. He shared many photos, memories and details about Antje.

Hilko had some original photographs and personal stories about his grandparents that nobody else in the world could have shared with us. In spite of the language barrier, we were able to have a very nice meeting and we left with more than we ever imagined in terms of stories, records and photographs of our ancestor, Antje Kap.

Another group of relatives (the Kiels and Waterbeeks) who attended the reception also brought along photos and fascinating memories of Antje. Between these two contacts, we gained valuable insights about her life. I have remained in contact with the Kiels and Waterbeeks and they have become good friends, in addition to being my third and fourth cousins.

TIP 56: Bring Pictures of Your Ancestors with You

It took me only a few minutes into my first visit to the Netherlands to recognize the value of bringing photos of my ancestors to share with local people, especially local relatives. I usually store these photos on my smartphone. The photographs are helpful in identifying common ancestors when I'm meeting with distant cousins. The relatives sometimes don't recognize a name when I say it, especially if I'm pronouncing it with my American accent, but they frequently recognize family members in old photographs.

Some of the relatives we met in Holland during the 2017 trip were surprised that we had photos of their grandparents and great-grandparents that they had never seen. They were extremely grateful as we gave them copies of these photos, both soft copies and hardcopy prints.

I also saved screenshots on my phone of pedigree charts of my ancestral lines from FamilySearch prior to the trip. These also came in handy several times in explaining the common ancestral connections with members of our tour group and the local relatives we met.

TIP 57: Churches and Church Meetings

It is common to find very old church buildings in large cities and small towns throughout Europe, with many dating back to the 17th century or earlier. These churches, which served as centers of community activities for centuries, often contain old records. Many churches also have cemeteries either on site or adjoining their properties. Records and cemeteries are always worth checking out, but those are not the only resources available at the churches in your ancestral homeland.

Church meetings can also be a great place to find family

history information. You may even meet members of your extended family by attending church meetings in your ancestral homeland. The Church of Jesus Christ of Latter-day Saints is especially effective in this regard, whether you are a member or not. If you *are* a member and you attend the church meetings in the area where your ancestors lived, you may even find distant relatives in the congregation. If not, it is likely that you will find people who know about your ancestors. You will also find that many in these congregations are passionate about family history research and are excited to share what they know.

It is not uncommon for members of a family to live in the same small town for hundreds of years in Europe. During my first trip to the Netherlands, my wife, daughter and I attended the Church of Jesus Christ of Latter-day Saints services in Groningen. The first person we met after walking into the church building introduced himself and said his name was Jan Dallinga. He was surprised when I replied, "Hello Jan. I'm related to you!"

I knew from the Dallinga surname in Groningen that we had common ancestors, and we quickly figured out the details of the connection. He then introduced me to his father, Kodinus, who was nearly 90 at the time. Kodinus, who recently passed away, proved to be a tremendously valuable source of information regarding my family and their experiences in the Netherlands before emigrating from Holland to America.

TIP 58: Combine Tourist Sites and Family-Specific Sites

In my experience, a combination of visiting well-known tourist sites along with some of the less-populated areas (if your family lived there) is the best approach for a trip to your ancestral homeland. During our trip in 2017, we found our three days in Amsterdam and the surrounding areas to be fascinating. Among the attractions we visited and enjoyed were the Anne Frank House, the Rijksmuseum, the Van Gogh museum, a canal boat tour, the Corrie Ten Boom House and the windmills of Kinderdijk.

Prior to the trip, most of our group members were especially excited to visit the tourist attractions. If we had not included the well-known places in the itinerary, fewer people would have joined the trip, so it was definitely a good decision to visit the tourist spots. Seeing the stark differences between life in Amsterdam versus the quaint villages of Groningen also gave us a good feel for the range of life experiences that were possible depending on where in Holland an ancestor may have lived.

However, as amazing as those famous attractions were, our favorite part of the trip was visiting the province of Groningen where we met many distant relatives and experienced the small towns where our ancestors lived.

TIP 59: Cemeteries in the Homeland

I have already highlighted the value of cemeteries as a resource in your family history research. While your time may be limited during a visit to your homeland, I strongly recommend visiting cemeteries if you can work it into your schedule. You should also do some research in advance to find where your ancestors are buried, which will make your visit much more efficient.

In our case, we visited one small cemetery in Schildwolde, Groningen, where we found several graves of ancestors which were not listed on findagrave.com, billiongraves.com or anywhere else. We were also able to piece together some fuzzy family relationships through the information we found on some of the headstones, so the hour we spent at that cemetery was very productive.

TIP 60: Don't Forget to Take Pictures!

This probably goes without saying, but be sure to take as many photographs as possible during your visit to the homeland. I've never met anybody who said they took too many photos during one of these trips, but I know many who have regretted their failure to take pictures of key places, people or other attractions.

I also recommend recording any conversations that you have with people who share information about your family. It is easy to get distracted by the excitement while visiting the various sites, forgetting to take pictures or record conversations. I also recommend bringing portable battery chargers for your smartphone so you don't miss the perfect photo opportunity because of a dead battery.

If you are traveling with a group, you can combine your efforts and upload and share all of your photographs online to a common site at the end of the trip. We used a Google Photos folder to share our pictures, but you can do the same thing through Dropbox, Facebook, or a variety of other sites.

LESSON 6

THE VALUE OF PHOTOS, VIDEO AND AUDIO

As I began researching my Dutch ancestry, I first reviewed a handful of stories and old photographs that my mother had received from her parents. Most of the photographs were of poor quality and many were damaged, but they still added a strong personal connection to my ancestors that I hadn't felt before. Eager to find more, I began searching much more intently for photographs of my ancestors.

Searching for old photographs and other media has become a primary focus of my research. On many occasions I've driven for hours just to have a chance to see and take pictures of a few old family photos.

My interest in finding photographs or other media is not only because of the flavor they can add to my research efforts. Old photographs, home movies and audio recordings are also by far the most widely appreciated things that I have shared with the extended family.

In addition to photographs and video, I have accumulated more than 1,000 hours of audio recordings from interviews with my elderly ancestors. These interviews are filled with wonderful stories and memories, offering insights into the many ways our ancestors influenced and blessed our lives.

Finding and sharing photos, video and audio recordings of

your ancestors will bring them to life, making them feel much more like the family members they are, and not just random names on a pedigree chart. In my experience, feeling that personal connection to my ancestors has been the most powerful motivator and the greatest blessing from doing this work. A list of names or a completed pedigree chart suddenly feels like something much more intimate as you learn who your ancestors were, and you begin to understand their lives and experiences in some detail.

Digitizing Photographs

I noted earlier that seeing old photographs can often spur memories, even for people with memory challenges. I have also highlighted that sharing photographs is an effective way to convince people to talk with you about their memories and to share whatever photographs they have of your common ancestors. Photographs also make any publication much more compelling and interesting to the reader. I have also found that hanging photos of my ancestors in my home can be inspiring.

Some of your old family photographs may be damaged, but there are people and resources available to improve and even restore severely damaged photographs. I found a member of the extended Kapp family who had experience in doing photo restoration and he was able to miraculously restore a particularly important photo for me.

TIP 61: Finding Photos on FamilySearch.org and Other Sites

For those with Western European ancestry, FamilySearch

contains a tremendous collection of photographs, especially if your Western European ancestors later immigrated to the Western United States. Just click on an ancestor's "person" page and then select "memories" to see any photos in the database for that person. The collection of photos and other "memories" in FamilySearch (including audio recordings) continues to grow, so check back periodically for new additions using the quick process I described in Tip 45. You can also find photographs on ancestry.com, findagrave.com, billiongraves.com, Fold3.com and many other sites.

TIP 62: Digitize Your Photos!

No matter how many old hard copy photos (prints) you have in your personal collection, your first step should be to digitize them. If the photographs are in reasonably good condition, this can be quickly and efficiently accomplished through the use of an auto-feed photo scanner.

Some traditional scanners can also do the trick. While not as fast as an auto-feed scanner, some advanced scanners will generate separate files for each photograph on the screen at once, saving you substantial time as compared to a traditional scanner which processes one photo at a time.

If you don't want to invest in an auto-feed scanner, there is also a software program called AutoSplitter which will automatically recognize multiple photographs on a scanned image, then crop and straighten them. AutoSplitter also has some color correction features and there is a free trial option. The software license is only $19.99 (a bargain!) so I highly recommend it if you have a lot of photos to scan and don't plan to purchase an auto-feed photo scanner.

You should use at least 300 DPI settings on your scanner for photos, but I would suggest 600 DPI if the photo is small and if you plan to enlarge the photo or include it in a book. I have created a YouTube video for Tip 62 that reviews some key features, benefits and options of auto-feed photo scanners as well as AutoSplitter. If you aren't interested in scanning your old photos yourself, there are companies that offer scanning services. You mail them your hard copy prints and they scan them for you.

TIP 63: Digitize Documents as Well

Investing in an auto-feed scanner can also save you a lot of time in digitizing old documents. Most auto-feed photo scanners can also scan a stack of printed pages very quickly. When combined with Optical Character Recognition (OCR) capabilities, the scanned pages can then be converted into digitized (searchable and editable) text in minutes or seconds. This capability has saved me countless hours that I would have otherwise spent transcribing documents.

TIP 64: What if Photos Are Fragile or Damaged?

If photographs are fragile or damaged, a traditional scanner is risky, and an auto-feed scanner is out of the question. I try to avoid handling fragile photographs altogether unless it is absolutely necessary. In such cases, photographing the old photos with your smartphone or a digital camera will usually work quite well to preserve the photo and make it usable for your genealogy efforts.

Keep in mind that the quality and resolution of old photographs is usually poor as compared to current standards, so you won't lose much, if anything, in terms of detail or photo quality by photographing them with a digital camera or a smartphone camera as long as the lighting is good and you avoid shadows and reflections.

Setting the photo up against a wall or object so it is vertical will usually give you better lighting results. Taking photos from above while the old photograph is lying flat on a table will often create shadows and glare, significantly reducing the quality of the digital image.

If you plan to use your smartphone to photograph a lot of photos, I highly recommend trying Google's PhotoScan app (for Android or iOS). It is easy to use and is especially good at reducing glare and reflections. See my YouTube video for Tip 64 to see a demonstration of the PhotoScan app.

TIP 65: Digitizing 35mm Slides or Negatives

35mm slides were a very popular medium for storing and sharing family photographs for several decades of the 20th century, so most families have large collections of slides unless somebody threw them away. The slide trays are bulky and slide projectors are increasingly rare, so this can be a cumbersome medium for accessing these photos for your family history research purposes. Fortunately, newer technology offers a solution to these problems.

A 35mm slide digitizer will allow you to quickly convert your old slides into digital photographs, usually with exceptional quality. There are quite a few options available, but most of them do the same basic job and do it equally well. I use a Magnasonic digitizer that I purchased on Amazon for about $70. In addition to 35mm slides, it will also convert negatives, 126KPK slides, 110 slides and Super 8 film (into digital photographs).

Kodak makes a similar product which is more expensive (about $160) but has similar features and is worth checking out. They also offer a cheaper option (about $39) which works with your smartphone camera.

It can be a bit laborious to convert a large group of slides on these devices because you do have to load each slide individually, but I was still able to convert several slides per minute using the feeder that was included with the Magnasonic. It is a cheap and flexible tool that works great for converting old, outdated slides into a usable digital format with excellent quality. I highly recommend using one of these devices if you have at least 100 old slides to convert. If you buy an advanced photo scanner (see Tip 62) it may also be capable of digitizing 35mm slides and negatives. My YouTube video for Tip 65 has more information.

Tip 66: Sorting, Organizing and Naming Your Digitized Photographs

Once you have your photos digitized, you will likely find yourself with hundreds if not thousands of photograph files on your computer. While I don't believe you can ever have too many photos in your collection, it can be very difficult to effectively manage and use a large collection of photos if it is not properly organized.

Organizing and naming these files can be a daunting task, but it doesn't have to be. It will save you an immense amount of time if you sort the photographs into groups and categories. You can use whatever organizing approach you wish, but I chose to organize photographs by family and individual and that has worked well.

My method is simple. I open File Explorer in Windows and use the "Extra Large Icon" view setting. I then drag and drop each photograph into a folder based on who is in the photo. You can drag and drop groups of photographs quite quickly, accomplishing this task much faster than you might expect. Once all of the photographs are in the proper folders, I then rename the photos within each folder with the name of the individual or the family, which now makes the photos "searchable."

This can also be done very quickly by naming all photos at once and letting Windows add the numbers to them automatically. While it is a bit difficult to explain this tip in text format, the process is easy to follow in my video for Tip 66 on the TechSmart Innovation YouTube channel.

Digitizing Video and Audio

Photographs are some of the most compelling records we have of our ancestors, but video, if you can find it, can be even more interesting and valuable. It should be noted, however, that video formats and storage media have changed and transitioned repeatedly over the past century and nearly every old home movie you find will require some form of digital conversion.

TIP 67: Digitizing 8mm or Super 8 Film

I have known several people who paid a company to convert 8mm or Super 8 film professionally and the results were good. However, this can be very expensive. I have one family member who has so many reels of film that the quote was several thousand dollars to convert them all, which made it cost prohibitive. If you are not sure what you have on each reel of film, it can also be disappointing to spend a lot of money, only to find that it was video that was not of any particular interest to you.

One low-cost alternative to professional digitization is to buy a film digitizer/converter. I purchased one on Amazon made by Wolverine. The machine does require a little babysitting, especially if the film is really old, but it works well and is easy to set up and use. I have converted several hours of video with the Wolverine and the results were good. I purchased the first-generation Wolverine for about $325. Wolverine now has a Pro model for about $400 that handles larger reels and produces higher resolution output.

If you are going to invest in one of these machines, I would go with the Pro model due to the improved quality and size flexibility benefits. You can also learn more about this method of video conversion through my YouTube video for Tip 67.

TIP 68: Digitizing Video from VHS Tapes

This one is pretty straightforward if you are fairly proficient with a computer. You will obviously need an old VCR/VHS tape player, which can be a bit difficult to find. I still see listings for VCR/DVD combo players, so that might be your best bet, especially if you ever had your old movies converted to DVD. I have saved a couple of old VHS players and they still work perfectly well.

With the VHS tape (or DVD) in the player, simply run the "out" signal from the player into your computer and record with one of the many video capture hardware/software options available. I have been doing this type of conversion for two decades now and the equipment today is much easier to use and cheaper than it was 15 or 20 years ago. I initially used a hardware device that converted the analog signal from the VHS player and then fed it into the computer. The device was expensive, the companion software was finicky and prone to crashing, and it didn't work very well.

There are now a variety of simple and cheap conversion devices available on Amazon and elsewhere which will allow you to run a video and audio signal from the VHS player directly into your computer through a USB port. You can then use one of many video capture software options to record the video that is playing on the screen. Nearly all video editing software programs include a capture function that can record video that comes in through an external feed in very high quality.

Ironically, you may find that the video quality of old 8mm film from the 1940s or 1950s that you convert is better than what you have on old VHS tapes from the 1970s and 1980s. All video stored on film will degrade over time, but VHS tends to be especially susceptible to degradation as it gets older. It will deteriorate even faster if it is not stored in dry, cool conditions. Please refer to my YouTube video for Tip 68 for step-by-step tips on digitizing your old VHS tapes.

Tip 69: Digitizing Audio from Cassette Tapes

I mentioned in Tip 2 that my mother and two of my uncles interviewed Aunt Grace when she was 96, and that the contents of that recording were an invaluable resource in my early efforts to learn about my Dutch ancestors. When I first listened to the recording years after it was recorded, the audio quality of the cassette was still good. However, my experience with cassette tapes included some that were melted and warped by the sun or eaten by a tape player, so I digitized the tape to make sure that this priceless recording wasn't lost.

I was also aware of a couple of cases where people in my family had preserved very old recordings of our ancestors on cassette. When we finally played the recordings, the sound quality had degraded so badly that they were no longer useful, so the information was lost.

As with photographs and video, you should prioritize

digitizing any audio cassette tapes as quickly as possible to preserve what is on them. While most people no longer have a cassette player in their home media system, you can still buy a cheap Walkman-type cassette player online. These players will generate a good enough signal to capture and preserve what is on a cassette tape, assuming the tape hasn't already degraded significantly.

This is an easy one to do. With the tape in the player, you connect a 3.55mm audio cable to the headphone jack on the cassette player, then plug the other end into the microphone jack of your computer. If your computer doesn't have a separate microphone jack (many new laptops don't), it should be configured for the headphone jack to also serve as the microphone jack. You may need a simple headphone and microphone plug adapter which can be purchased on Amazon for about $8.00, but many will work without that.

With the cassette player connected to your computer, you can use any audio capture software to record the incoming audio signal. I have used a software program called TotalRecorder (by High Criteria) for more than a decade, and it works great. High Criteria offers a basic version for about $15 or a professional edition for $35.

If you want to get more serious and do some manipulation of the sound, the professional edition is worth the investment. High Criteria also offers more expensive versions which include audio restoration and speech enhancement features.

There are also various free software programs available online that will record incoming audio if you want to go that route. I have converted hundreds of hours of audio, so investing $35 in the software was a wise move in my case. You can also see how to do this on my YouTube video for Tip 69.

LESSON 7

FILING AND ORGANIZING YOUR DIGITAL RECORDS

While this may not be the most exciting lesson in the book, it might save you more time and frustration than you ever expected, especially as your collection of files and records grows over time.

As I have noted previously, my archive of family history records now includes over 65,000 files and occupies roughly 200GB of memory on my hard drive. Even with a collection this large, I can almost always find any file, photograph or record that I need within a few seconds, and I can do that from home, work, or while I am on the road. This is because I have employed an effective system for filing and organizing my records.

I should note here that when I began this work in earnest, I never anticipated that I would acquire and archive so much information. I also know that I am not alone in that regard. Most people eventually collect enough information that it becomes challenging to organize. A failure to organize your information also makes it much more difficult to share your family history findings with others. The tips in this chapter will help you to keep your record archive manageable and nimble, regardless of how large it becomes, enabling you to access and share it without much effort.

TIP 70: Organizing Your Digitized Files into Folders

I previously described the importance of organizing your photographs into folders, whether that organizing is done by family, name, year or some other criteria. You should do the same with all of your digitized genealogy records and files, not just photographs.

I have learned that it is also extremely helpful to name each file with a term that is searchable, whether it is the name of the individual(s) referenced in the record or perhaps the date or location of the record. I didn't do this initially and regretted that decision, so I went back and re-named everything.

Having intelligent names for each file allows you to search for them very quickly. This has been a lifesaver for me with over 65,000 records on my computer. You can also view my YouTube video for Tips 70 and 71 on how to rename files very quickly and efficiently, just as I showed with photographs.

TIP 71: File Naming and Chronological Timelines

I begin most file names with the file or record date in the format of year-month-day (YYYY-MM-DD), and I may add additional details after that. I might also employ my group renaming function here. By including the actual record date at the beginning of the file name, it is very easy to quickly assemble a chronological timeline of your ancestor's life.

While including the date may feel like overkill, it is very easy to sort files by year or even by year and month and then rename the files all at once (as I have shown previously with photos and other files). Again, you can refer to the TechSmart Innovation YouTube channel for a quick demonstration of how to do this in the video for Tips 70 and 71.

Sorting files into chronological order is also ideal for efficient storytelling. After researching your ancestors' lives, your next objective should be to document and share what you have learned. If you tell your ancestors' story in an interesting, compelling way, there will be a lot more interest and response than if you simply offer a huge ancestor information dump with no storyline. If your file names begin with dates, it is much easier to assemble and tell the life story of your ancestors.

Ask yourself, would you rather read a story book or a phone book? A list of ancestor names and dates with no photos, stories or context will feel a lot like a phone book to the reader. A story is always better than a phone book.

TIP 72: Making Your Record Archive Portable and Accessible

I initially stored all of my files on my home computer. It was an effective approach, and I still think it is a good idea to have one "master" copy of your records. However, information on my home computer was not always easily accessible when I was away from home.

I then began using different cloud-based storage options so I could access files no matter where I was. I have primarily used Google Drive for storing my files in the cloud, but I have also used Dropbox and Microsoft OneDrive at times. There are many other cloud storage services available, all of which offer the same basic functionality for free or a very low cost. Whatever you use, I recommend replicating the folder, file and naming format from your home computer files on the cloud storage service to keep things consistent.

Cloud-based storage is great, but I have also experienced the frustration of not being able to access a cloud-based storage site due to a lack of internet service or some other technical problem, so I also maintain a copy of all key records on a portable storage device which I can carry with me when I am traveling. I have used a variety of SD cards, USB drives and external hard drives for this purpose and they have also worked great in allowing me to access my records when I'm traveling. The 512GB SD cards and USB drives are very affordable (and also compact) so you can easily carry a huge archive in one of these devices and it won't cost you much at all. By using a simple backup program, you can keep these external devices current.

You also have the option of saving any new photos or records that you find during your travels to the portable storage device. If you do that (and you probably will), I highly recommend saving everything to a "working" folder on that SD card or USB drive so you can quickly move it to your master file on the home computer and/or cloud service to keep everything aligned and synchronized.

TIP 73: Sharing, Copying or Transferring Records

I am frequently asked to share some of my files with relatives or others whom I meet. I've found that technology can make this a simple, quick and seamless process.

If somebody asks for a copy of a set of records and that set is too large to email, I usually share the files with them from my Google Drive. One benefit of using the Google Drive option is that you can put security controls on the file or folders, restricting who can access them and whether or not they can edit the file(s).

I have also used SD cards or USB drives to transfer large files or archives to others if we are in the same physical location. I frequently use this method at family reunions.

In addition, I have used the Google Drive app capability on the iPhone to quickly move large files into Google Drive where I can then access the information. This is another tip that is a bit difficult to describe in text format without a very long description, but you can view the YouTube video for Tip 73 to see how simple and easy this one can be.

One note about cloud-based storage solutions: I know some people are strong believers in storing all of their information on a cloud site such as Google Drive, even making that their primary storage location. I am admittedly a bit paranoid, but after seeing people who lost records or found themselves unable to access their files when they didn't have internet access, I always maintain my primary archive on my home computer with multiple backups. I do this not only for accessibility purposes but also security concerns, as some of the information can be sensitive.

I won't go into any more detail on this one here, but I plan to include a lot more information on this topic in a future book called *Power Tools for Family History Research*, which will focus exclusively on the application of technology in this work.

TIP 74: Remote Desktop Software

Even if you effectively utilize the tools and solutions listed earlier in this chapter, there may be times where you find yourself in a remote location and you wish you had access to your full home computer instead of what you have stored in the cloud or on your portable storage devices.

Remote desktop software programs offer the solution to that problem. These tools, many of which are free, will allow you to access your home computer remotely from any internet or cellular data connection via a computer or even a smartphone. With a remote connection to your home computer, you can directly control it and access any files or programs you may need.

There are various remote desktop programs available, and

you can find several through a quick Google search for "remote desktop software." I have personally used TeamViewer as my remote desktop solution for many years now. TeamViewer has been a leading option for a long time and it is very easy to use. It is also free and can be used from either a computer or a smartphone. You can search for "TeamViewer demo" on YouTube or Google for a quick tutorial on how it works.

TIP 75: Spreadsheets of Key Information and Facts

As your archive becomes large, you may find, like I did, that having a quick, sortable spreadsheet of key data or information can save you a lot of time. Even if your file names are searchable, there is a faster way to catalog key information sources which you use frequently.

For my most frequently used records and files, I have created a handful of spreadsheets with key information. These spreadsheets contain a wealth of useful details about my primary ancestors, including names, key dates in their lives, addressees, employment history, immigration details, spouses, children, etc. I have populated these spreadsheets with data going back as far as 200 years in some cases.

Moving this information into a spreadsheet makes the information quickly searchable, sortable, and filterable. It can also allow you to do other interesting things with your information. For example, my spreadsheet of ancestor addresses allowed me to generate a map of every home in the city of Ogden, Utah where my ancestors lived between 1899 and 1960. It was fascinating to see how frequently members of the extended family lived in the same neighborhoods, streets, and even the same homes in some cases. I have shared some examples of how this works and how I compiled the map in my video for Tip 75 posted on the YouTube channel.

Here is a list of some of the spreadsheets I have created to summarize key information found in my records:

- Research sources (website descriptions and URLs)
- Ancestor burial details, including cemetery names and burial plot locations
- Ancestor immigration dates and details
- A catalog of audio interviews with elderly relatives, including date, topics covered, time index of the recording and transcription status
- Contact names, emails and phone numbers for relatives (very useful for organizing family reunions)
- Ancestor addresses and occupations by year (from city directories) - described in Tip 28

TIP 76: Genealogy Software

As you assemble more and more information about your family, you will also find that keeping track of your ancestors can become a challenge. While many people utilize a personal pedigree chart in ancestry.com or a public pedigree chart or a private user-submitted "genealogy" in FamilySearch.org, the best option in my experience is a dedicated genealogy database program.

I have used several over the years, but RootsMagic is the best of those I've tried. RootsMagic is robust, fairly easy to learn, flexible and it interfaces seamlessly with the major online genealogy databases like ancestry.com and FamilySearch.org. It will also interface well with the files you store on your computer. While some people prefer to store all of their photos, records and documents inside RootsMagic itself, I believe it is better to be more selective in that regard if you have an especially large collection of records, like I do.

LESSON 8

VOICE RECOGNITION SOFTWARE AND TRANSLATION TOOLS

When I began my initial outline for this book, I planned to include some tips about voice recognition software and translation tools, but I didn't expect to dedicate an entire chapter to these two topics. However, the more I used these tools, the more obvious it became that they are some of the most powerful and useful capabilities available to genealogists, and their usefulness continues to grow.

As I noted earlier, time can be your friend or your foe. If you use your time wisely and efficiently, it becomes your friend, offering you even more time to do research and other interesting and enjoyable aspects of this work. Conversely, if you use your time inefficiently, you will find that your progress will slow, your frustrations will increase and the joy you receive from the work will decrease.

Various studies have shown that the average person speaks at a rate of about 150 words per minute, which is roughly five times faster than the average person types on a keyboard, and 12 times faster than writing by hand.

Translating that into more practical terms, if you were working on a 200-page (60,000-word) book about your ancestors, and you had your information all researched, summarized and organized into an outline, it would take you just under 6.7 hours to dictate it, 33 hours to type it, or 80 hours to write it by hand. When you have a lot of words to put into text, dictation is by far the most efficient method available. In fact, I wrote (dictated) most of this book using voice recognition software.

Dramatic improvements in the quality, affordability and availability of voice recognition (dictation) software in recent years makes this a much more useful tool than most people realize. You may not have plans to write a book or to undertake anything on that scale, but there are still many uses for voice recognition software in your genealogy work. The tips below offer just a few examples of how this technology tool can be of use.

TIP 77: Use Dictation to Make Your Story More Interesting

While there are exceptions, a person's speaking style is frequently more interesting and entertaining than his or her writing style. This is especially true with talented speakers and storytellers, where some of the personality and charisma that makes them such compelling communicators is lost when a story is written instead of told. By using voice recognition software to document the history of your ancestors, you don't lose that unique "personality" that comes out when you tell a good story.

TIP 78: A Wide Range of Devices and Options

For many years, voice recognition software was only available on personal computers and it wasn't particularly accurate, which limited its usefulness. Powerful, accurate voice recognition software is now available in various formats and on a wide range of devices, including virtually any desktop computer, laptop, tablet or smartphone, making the technology especially flexible and convenient. I first began using voice recognition software on a desktop computer, which was somewhat useful. As I found versions that worked on laptops and then smartphones over the years, the software became much more useful in my family history work.

The availability of voice recognition software on smartphones has made it convenient and affordable for millions of people worldwide, multiplying its potential benefits. There are numerous dictation apps available for smartphones, including many that are cheap or even free.

So, which option should you use? In my experience, Dragon Naturally Speaking software is by far the most accurate (amazingly so), but it's also the most expensive, especially the mobile version which currently requires a subscription. However, if you expect to do a lot of dictation, I would invest the money for Dragon. You will be surprised at how accurate it is, especially as you fine tune it over time.

If you're not ready to invest in Dragon but you want a solution for your desktop or laptop computer, Google Docs includes a "Voice Typing" feature that is fairly accurate and is also free. It is not as robust nor as accurate as Dragon Naturally Speaking, but it can still be quite useful. Voice Typing can be accessed in a Google document by clicking the "Tools" menu item at the top of the page, then selecting "Voice Typing."

TIP 79: Keeping Your Dictation Files Synchronized

If you're like me, you'll find that voice recognition software is more useful than you expected, and you'll use it more and more as you try it for different use cases. I soon found that I was generating dictated files on my desktop computer, my laptops (I have a few) and my smartphone, sometimes all in the same day. I recognized that I needed a process to combine and consolidate these files and to keep them organized. I went with a Google Drive approach, and it has allowed me to seamlessly add and combine my dictations for a certain topic into a single storage location or even a single document.

Dragon software has its own dictation output window, or you can use any other text program as the output location of your dictation. To minimize transfers, I use a Microsoft Word document as my dictation output window for Dragon.

That isn't an option for my smartphone dictation since I'm too cheap to pay for the mobile subscription for Dragon, so I use another dictation app called "Dictate," and then copy the output with a single click and paste it into my document with a second click. If I happen to be in a location without internet access, I can copy the dictated text and paste it into a new note (using the iPhone "Notes" app) which can then be copied to the document once I have a connection.

Explaining this without a video demonstration is a bit clunky, but my YouTube videos for Tip 73 and Tip 78 should help you out with this one as well.

TIP 80: Make Your Commute Time Productive!

For most of my professional life I have spent about two hours per day commuting. Even if you spend an hour or two per week on your commute, or if you have other unproductive down time on a regular basis, I encourage you to use voice recognition software to make this a productive time to do family history work.

I find myself using smartphone-based voice recognition apps more and more frequently, even though they are not as accurate as the more powerful and expensive software I use on my laptop or desktop. With dictation software, I can now use those open windows of time to do some "writing" or to jot down plans for my next round of research. Another benefit of smartphone dictation apps is that you can start dictating within a few seconds of picking up your phone.

Even if you're only able to spend 15 minutes dictating during your commute, the amount of text generated in those 15 minutes would have taken more than an hour to type on a keyboard, and over three hours to write by hand. My smartphone app will never be my primary dictation tool, but it is a great secondary option for when I can't use Dragon.

TIP 81: Improve Your Dictation Accuracy for Maximum Benefits

I have met a few people who said the accuracy of their voice recognition output was so bad that they stopped using it. In each case, I found that they were either using outdated software or they were missing one or more key factors to ensure maximum accuracy. Those factors include:

1. Which App or Program: The better the program, the more accurate the results will be, which is why I recommend a robust program like Dragon Naturally Speaking if you want highly accurate output. Some benefits of Dragon include:

    a. Learning Your Voice: When you set up your Dragon software, it will ask you to read a series of phrases and it will then "learn" your voice, including your accent.

    b. Microphone Calibration: When you set up the Dragon microphone, it accounts for the noise level of the place where you set it up. If you move to a new location and the background noise is different, you can recalibrate the microphone and it will improve the accuracy of your dictation.

c. Add Words to the Vocabulary: If Dragon consistently gets a word wrong, that word is likely not in its vocabulary. You can add the word to the vocabulary, avoiding the need to edit or type the word in the future.

2. Which Device: The same pattern is true here as with the software application. The better the device you are using, especially the microphone on the device, the more accurate your output will be. When people are getting especially bad results on a smartphone, it is often because the microphone they are using is in their earbuds and is of low quality. The best output I have achieved is on my laptop with Dragon software and the Dragon headset that came with the software.

3. Background Noise: This is a common challenge if you are dictating to your smartphone while driving, riding a bus or train, or you are in some other noisy environment. Using a headset is one way to minimize background noise.

4. Speak Slowly and Clearly: The more slowly you speak and the more clearly you enunciate your words, the better the accuracy will be. Anyone who has learned a foreign language understands this principle. Even if you learn a language well in classes, the speed of a native speaker is often the greatest challenge to understanding. Voice recognition software will understand you much better if you speak slowly and enunciate each word clearly.

TIP 82: Transcribe Previously Recorded Interviews

I noted at the outset of the book that interviewing your elderly relatives is perhaps the most critical first step in documenting your family history. These interviews generate fascinating stories and information, but transcribing the interviews is a LOT of work. I have not found any voice recognition software that is capable of transcribing a two-person interview "live" with much accuracy, let alone a previously recorded conversation. However, voice recognition software can still help you to significantly speed up the transcription process.

If you listen to the completed interview on headphones, you can repeat it back out loud as you listen to it. With the voice recognition software "transcribing" the interview from your voice, you can speed up the transcription process significantly. This method is not quite as efficient as a live transcription and you will likely have to pause every few sentences, but this is still much faster than transcribing an interview by typing it out word for word.

TIP 83: Journaling Made Easy!

Even if you're not writing a book or creating any other significant text-based document as part of your genealogy work, voice recognition software can still help you. At the very least, you should use this technology to write your personal journal or record your own life history. I'm confident that anyone who spends any serious time doing genealogy will agree that our research today would be easier if more of our ancestors had been diligent in keeping journals. Only a few of my ancestors did much in this regard, but I am so grateful for those who did.

You should do your part for future generations by

recording the story of your life, even if you don't believe your life has been "interesting" or worthy of recording. In ten hours or less, you can sit down at your computer and create a rough outline of your life, highlighting key events from each year, decade or phase of life. You can then use that outline to tell the story of your life by simply talking about your memories of the key events included in the timeline, recording it all with voice recognition software. Whether you think your life is noteworthy or not, that history will likely become a treasure to future generations.

TIP 84: Translation Tools

The same technology advancements that have made voice recognition powerful, affordable and accessible have also enabled great strides in language translation. Google has been a leader in this area for some time, and I have gravitated toward their solutions because they are robust, available on a range of devices and they are free. That's a difficult combination to beat. Google's suite of translation tools includes the following:

1. <u>Smartphone App</u>: I probably use this one most frequently, but mostly for understanding specific words or phrases that I come across in my genealogy research. It is not ideal for long text translations, but it works great for short items. It is also extremely useful if you are traveling to an ancestral homeland where you don't speak the language. Not only will it allow you to translate words into English quickly and accurately, it will also allow you to speak English into the app which will then translate your words into the foreign language of your choice. As Google notes, you can "speak, snap, write or type" the words that you

want translated, which is really impressive. Google Translate (at least the Android version) can also be combined with any other app, translating the text within that app.

2. <u>Computer Version</u>: For large bodies of text, I strongly prefer the website version of Google Translate found at http://translate.google.com. The tool offers over 100 languages if you input the text by typing (far fewer languages if you write, talk or snap), and a computer keyboard is always a more efficient interface for typing text than a smartphone screen.

3. <u>Website Translator</u>: From the same computer version of Google Translate noted above, you can also enter the URL for a website published in a foreign language (in the box on the left). Make sure the "detect" language is set to the foreign language of the website, then a URL will appear in the English box on the right. Click on that URL and you will see the website translated into English, with a toggle button in the upper right to switch back to the original language if you wish. This is an especially powerful tool if you find a website, database or catalog of genealogy information from your ancestral homeland that is only available in a foreign language. The translations are never perfect, but they are typically close enough to give you a good understanding of the information found on the site.

LESSON 9

THE VALUE OF FORMAL TRAINING

As noted earlier, my grandfather was a prolific genealogist and he shared a lot of his work with me. He also trained me to do genealogy work the way he did it. While he had worked with some professional genealogists in the Family History Library in Salt Lake City Utah, he was mostly self-taught, and that didn't seem to hinder his efforts.

I had extensive experience in the tech industry when my interest in genealogy was re-kindled. In addition, I had worked as a research professional in the business world and I had been an adjunct university professor, so I was comfortable doing in-depth research in a variety of realms. I had also helped other people with their family history research, and I was familiar with many of the tools described in this book.

So, based on my work experience, and the fact that so much of modern genealogy research is done via technology, I wrongfully assumed that formal training wouldn't really help me. While I did an adequate job before I was certified, I learned valuable information and techniques through earning a certification.

For those who are very serious about doing genealogy research but are skeptical of formal training (as I was), I will list a few of the key benefits in the subsequent tips.

TIP 85: Determining the Reliability of Source Information

Not all sources of genealogy information are created equal. In fact, many of the sources you'll find are questionable at best, so it is necessary to understand the rules and standards by which genealogy sources are categorized. I won't attempt to explain the various categories and standards here, as there are many factors to consider, but you can gain a valuable understanding of source validity and how to determine the credibility of sources by pursuing and completing formal training or certification.

TIP 86: Paleography

As I began my certification process, a friend who was pursuing the same certification recommended a course in paleography. He said it was by far the most difficult genealogy course he had taken, but also the most useful. He was right on both counts.

Paleography is the study of ancient handwriting and historical documents. This was likely the most valuable course in my certification course work.

An example of handwriting taken from a vital record from Essex County, Massachusetts in the early 1700s

Since most old records are hand-written, and handwriting varies dramatically across time periods and geographic regions, you may need to recognize and understand the handwriting, scripts, and documents from various time periods and countries. Formal training in paleography is included as part of any credentialed or accredited certification program and will give you the proper training to read and understand old records.

TIP 87: New Research Sources, Tools and Techniques:

My formal certification as a family history researcher also exposed me to a long list of research sources and tools that I doubt I would have found on my own. Examples include repositories of wills, probate records, county records, various microfilm and microfiche sources, and numerous online sources for obscure or narrowly focused record types. I also learned many useful research techniques from my professors and the materials in my certification program.

TIP 88: Record Preservation Techniques and Practices

Most genealogist either have or will eventually acquire a collection of old, hardcopy records. These records, which may contain the most valuable information in your archive, will deteriorate over time until they eventually become difficult or impossible to read.

However, you can minimize that deterioration and extend the life of those records by storing and handling them properly. This is another area where my formal training gave me valuable insights. I explained in the introduction that my grandfather left me a large collection of family records. This collection includes some documents that are nearly 200 years old. My certification program explained the best storage environment and techniques for preserving such documents.

TIP 89: Certification Adds Credibility

Earning a certification or credential in genealogy research will also give you credibility that may be useful when you are seeking access to records or information. It confirms to others that you take your work seriously and that you have invested the time and effort to learn proper methods. Some of the professional genealogists I have worked with were more willing to collaborate and share records with me once they learned that I was a certified researcher myself.

Perhaps you are interested in pursuing a certification or accreditation, but you're not sure where to start. The two most popular accreditation organizations are the Board for Certification of Genealogists (BCG) and the International Commission for the Accreditation of Professional Genealogists (ICAPGen). A quick Google search will give you a detailed list of their respective requirements. Both organizations base their certifications on research that you submit for review.

You can also earn a certification or even a bachelor's degree in genealogy through various universities, including some that offer online programs which are especially convenient and increasingly popular.

An accreditation, certification or credential is almost always necessary if you want to do professional or paid research, but I believe the knowledge you gain in the process is the greatest benefit.

LESSON 10

FIND YOUR NICHE

Gaining a solid understanding of the basics in each area or discipline of genealogy is important and recommended. You can gain this foundation most effectively through a good certification or degree program or through reading books and taking classes. However, you will soon recognize, as I did, that family history is an extremely broad area of study with many different areas of specialization. Becoming an expert in even one or two of these areas may require years or decades of time investment. But don't let that discourage you. You can become very proficient and effective in doing your own family history research without becoming an expert in any specific area.

TIP 90: Choose Your Focus Area(s)

A broad foundation is a great start and is necessary, but if you plan to make this a serious endeavor or even a long-term hobby, I recommend that you choose your specialization niche(s). I always suggest that people focus their long-term efforts in one or two areas rather than attempt to become an expert in everything. I've found that those who pursue one or two key focus areas tend to enjoy the work more, and they also have more success in accomplishing their goals.

If you want to become a great baseball player, you wouldn't try to become a great infielder, outfielder, catcher *and* pitcher. Even at a young age, players usually specialize. That is because the skills required to excel in baseball vary from position to position. The same concept applies here.

I personally faced this dilemma early on. I determined fairly soon that my greatest enjoyment and accomplishments came from discovering and documenting the life stories of my ancestors.

I have also enjoyed finding ways to apply new technology to genealogy work. I then used that knowledge to begin training and teaching others, which has also become an especially rewarding part of the work. I still do other aspects of genealogy work, but my primary focus is on storytelling, technology application and training others.

Others may prefer a more technical focus, with a specialization in paleography or documents from a certain region or time period. If you plan to invest a significant amount of time in this work, but you are unsure as to where you should focus your efforts, begin with these questions: What aspect of the work do you really love? Of the work you have done so far, what brings you the greatest excitement and joy? If you've found yourself staying up late and not wanting to stop, what kind of genealogy work were you doing?

I have one good friend who loves to extract names and information about his ancestors from old records, and he has made this his primary focus. By concentrating on that aspect of the work he has gained an immense understanding of vital and public records from dozens of countries and sources. He is a go-to expert for this area of genealogy and I have relied on his expertise many times.

I have another friend who is a respected expert on Dutch genealogy and records. He is fluent in Dutch, he has lived in the Netherlands and he leads a research organization focused on Dutch research. He has been an invaluable resource in my efforts, and he loves the area he has chosen to focus on.

TIP 91: Set Specific Goals Within Your Focus Area(s)

Once you decide on the area or areas that bring you the greatest satisfaction, you should then set goals and write them down. What do you want to accomplish or learn first in this area? Make that initial goal your priority and focus your time on it until you have accomplished your goal.

By focusing on completing a series of short-term (1-3 month) goals which are not overly ambitious, you will be on your way to achieving more significant long-term (1-2 year) goals. A list of long-term goals might include:

- Completing pedigree charts for your ancestors
- Writing the life story of an ancestor
- Mastering a new genealogy software program (i.e., RootsMagic) or research database (ancestry.com or FamilySearch.org)
- Gathering, digitizing and organizing a collection of photos, documents or other records
- Researching the genealogy of a specific geographic region where your ancestors lived
- Gathering work for church purposes (this one is common among members of the Church of Jesus Christ of Latter-day Saints)

TIP 92: Be Flexible!

Whatever area you decide to focus on, my suggestion is to be flexible in your research plan. Don't get hung up on one missing name, date or record. I always keep a "bin list" of items that I am unable to find after a reasonable amount of research. When I have hit a persistent challenge like this, I move on to something else and come back and give these bin list items another shot at a later date.

I have met with many people who became frustrated with their family history work because they were unable to find a single record, date or fact. It is easy to become obsessed with that single item, and that usually results in a lot of wasted time and unnecessary frustration. There are always other avenues, records and ancestors to explore, so pick one of those and put that problematic item in your personal bin list to research later.

I learned this lesson the hard way. I searched in vain for the birth and death records of one of my great-great-grandmothers who was born in England. I worked on it at least weekly for nearly a year, but found nothing. I finally set it aside and decided to come back to it another time. A year or two later, a random phone call from my dad after he and my mom had visited a cemetery gave me the little clue I needed, and within a few hours I had the records that had eluded me.

TIP 93: Let Indexing Fill in Your Research Gaps

On multiple occasions I have searched in vain for a record that apparently did not exist at the time I began my search, only to find that the record became available months or years later. This is not uncommon. With hundreds of millions of new records being indexed and made available online each year, the catalog of records is constantly expanding.

I remember many people saying in the 1980s and 1990s that their genealogy work was "done" based on the work completed at that time. In many cases that was true in the sense that they or their relatives had exhausted all records and sources available at that time. However, the incredible growth of worldwide indexing efforts has changed all of that. When somebody tells me today that their work is done, I always assure them that it is not. I have yet to be proven wrong.

A good example to demonstrate this fact comes from my experience with a friend named Howard. Some members of Howard's family had done extensive research into their family lines in the preceding decades. He had been told by some experienced researchers in his family years earlier that their work was "done," so he figured he had nothing left to find. When he told me this, I assured him that we could find new information and records about his family, and that his family's work was definitely not done.

Howard agreed to come by the Family History Center (where I am the director) the following Tuesday evening, but he didn't show up. When he arrived the next Tuesday, he apologized for missing the previous week, explaining that he had been held up by an unexpected water leak in his ceiling the previous Tuesday night. We dove into the records and soon found dozens of new names and hundreds of accompanying records for his ancestors which were not included in his existing pedigree charts.

Howard was both happy and surprised to find these records, realizing that his work was definitely not done. As we looked more closely at the new information behind the records, I showed him that they had just been made available that week. If he had stopped by the previous Tuesday as planned, the new records would not yet have been available. So, the water leak in his ceiling turned out to be a blessing in disguise, at least from a family history standpoint.

TIP 94: Who Will Benefit from Your Work?

If you are still unsure as to what area you want to focus on, you should also ask yourself what you hope to accomplish or produce as a result of your time investment in this work. If the primary beneficiary of your research is yourself, that is fine, but I think you will have missed an immense opportunity to also benefit others in your family.

I began my own research with my personal goals as the primary objective, but I soon learned that hundreds and perhaps thousands of others in my extended family also had a strong interest in what I was seeking. I realized that if I produced something to benefit all of them, I could dramatically expand the impact and value of my work.

Whatever path you pursue, it will likely require a substantial investment of time and effort, and perhaps money as well. With that in mind, you should be thoughtful as to your objectives, goals and what you hope to produce. Write them down and track your progress.

If you are reading this book, it is likely that you already feel compelled, perhaps by some unknown force, to do genealogy research. This is common and exciting! The best results come to those who are passionate and feel driven to do this work.

One of my primary objectives in writing the book was to help those people who feel this compelling desire to research their family history. I am confident that by applying the methods described here, you can improve your efficiency and effectiveness. My confidence is based on the fact that I've seen each of these 10 lessons and 94 tips benefit various people with whom I have worked.

In closing, I encourage you to check out the Facebook page, website and YouTube channel listed on the following page for more information about the topics covered in the book. I look forward to interacting with you there! And if you liked the book, please give it a good review on Amazon!

MORE INFORMATION

Facebook: http://fb.me/Genealogy101Book

A great place to ask questions, interact with the author and provide feedback on the book, the YouTube videos or anything else.

Website: http://TechSmartInnovation.com

*Family history information can be found under the **Publishing**, **Training** and **Research** menu items at the top of the home page.*

YouTube Channel: Search for the "TechSmart Innovation" channel at YouTube.com

Here you'll find step-by-step video demonstrations of many of the tips from the book. If you'd like to see a video of something that isn't already there, let me know and I'll add it!

ABOUT THE AUTHOR

Jedd K. Parkinson has personally trained and assisted thousands of people with their genealogy research over the past decade. After receiving repeated requests for a manual containing his lessons and tips, Mr. Parkinson decided to put them all into this handbook. He has supplemented the book with a series of YouTube videos providing step-by-step instructions for many of the tips contained in this volume.

Mr. Parkinson has worked in the technology industry since 1997 as a people leader and supply chain strategist. Through that work he's enjoyed the unique opportunity of contributing directly to the launching and manufacturing of many of the game-changing technologies and products that have transformed genealogy research in recent years. In addition to his work in the tech industry, he has been an adjunct university professor for more than a decade.

Mr. Parkinson earned his Certification in Family History Research from Brigham Young University Idaho in 2016. He also holds a bachelor's degree from Weber State University (Summa Cum Laude and Valedictorian) and an MBA from Brigham Young University with additional postgraduate work done through Cornell University.

An author of five books with others in the works, Mr. Parkinson is a frequent speaker at family history meetings, training classes, firesides and other events organized by church or community groups. He and his wife Lisa are the parents of five children. He can be contacted at jeddparkinson@yahoo.com.

www.ingramcontent.com/pod-product-compliance
Lightning Source LLC
Chambersburg PA
CBHW070116300326
41934CB00035B/1353